Your Personal Horoscope 2019

Taurus

Your Personal Horoscope 2019

Taurus

21st April–21st May

igloobooks

igloobooks

Published in 2018
by Igloo Books Ltd
Cottage Farm
Sywell
NN6 0BJ
www.igloobooks.com

Produced for Igloo Books by Foulsham Publishing Ltd, The Old Barrel Store,
Drayman's Lane, Marlow, Bucks SL7 2FF, England

FIR003 0718
2 4 0 0 10 9 7 5 3 1
ISBN: 978-1-78810-564-4

This is an abridged version of material originally published
in Old Moore's Horoscope and Astral Diary.

Cover designed by Nicholas Gage
Edited by Bobby Newlyn-Jones

Printed and manufactured in China

CONTENTS

INTRODUCTION

Your personal horoscopes have been specifically created to allow you to get the most from astrological patterns and the way they have a bearing on not only your zodiac sign, but nuances within it. Using the diary section of the book you can read about the influences and possibilities of each and every day of the year. It will be possible for you to see when you are likely to be cheerful and happy or those times when your nature is in retreat and you will be more circumspect. The diary will help to give you a feel for the specific 'cycles' of astrology and the way they can subtly change your day-to-day life. For example, when you see the sign ☿, this means that the planet Mercury is retrograde at that time. Retrograde means it appears to be running backwards through the zodiac. Such a happening has a significant effect on communication skills, but this is only one small aspect of how the personal horoscope can help you.

With your personal horoscope the story doesn't end with the diary pages. It includes simple ways for you to work out the zodiac sign the Moon occupied at the time of your birth, and what this means for your personality. In addition, if you know the time of day you were born, it is possible to discover your Ascendant, yet another important guide to your personal make-up and potential.

Many readers are interested in relationships and in knowing how well they get on with people of other astrological signs. You might also be interested in the way you appear to very different sorts of individuals. If you are such a person, the section on Venus will be of particular interest. Despite the rapidly changing position of this planet, you can work out your Venus sign, and learn what bearing it will have on your life.

Using your personal horoscope you can travel on one of the most fascinating and rewarding journeys that anyone can take – the journey to a better realisation of self.

THE ESSENCE
OF TAURUS

Exploring the Personality of Taurus the Bull

(21ST APRIL – 21ST MAY)

What's in a sign?

Taurus is probably one of the most misunderstood signs of the zodiac. Astrologers from the past described those born under the sign of the Bull as being gentle, artistic, stubborn and refined. All of this is quite true, but there is so much more to Taureans and the only reason it isn't always discussed as much as it should be is because of basic Taurean reserve. Taureans are generally modest, and don't tend to assert themselves in a direct sense, unless in self-defence. As a result the sign is often sidelined, if not ignored.

You know what you want from life and are quite willing to work long and hard to get it. However, Taurus is also a great lover of luxury, so when circumstances permit you can be slow, ponderous and even lax. If there is a paradox here it is merely typical of Venus-ruled Taurus. On differing occasions you can be chatty or quiet, bold or timorous, smart or scruffy. It all depends on your commitment to a situation. When you are inspired there is nobody powerful enough to hold you back and when you are passionate you have the proclivities of a Casanova!

There are aspects of your nature that seldom change. For example, you are almost always friendly and approachable, and invariably have a sense of what feels and looks just right. You are capable and can work with your hands as well as your brain. You don't particularly care for dirt or squalid surroundings, preferring cleanliness, and you certainly don't take kindly to lowly settings. Most Taureans prefer the country to the coast, find loving relationships easy to deal with and are quite committed to home and family.

Whilst variety is the spice of life to many zodiac signs, this is not necessarily the case for Taurus. Many people born under the sign of the Bull remain happy to occupy a specific position for years on end.

9

It has been suggested, with more than a grain of truth, that the only thing that can get the Bull moving on occasions is a strategically placed bomb. What matters most, and which shows regularly in your dealings with the world at large, is your innate kindness and your desire to help others.

Taurus resources

The best word to describe Taurean subjects who are working to the best of their ability would be 'practical'. Nebulous situations, where you have to spend long hours thinking things through in a subconscious manner, don't suit you half as much as practical tasks, no matter how complex these might be. If you were to find yourself cast up on a desert island you would have all the necessities of life sorted out in a flash. This is not to suggest that you always recognise this potential in yourself. The problem here is that a very definite lack of self-belief is inclined to make you think that almost anyone else in the world has the edge when it comes to talent.

Another of your greatest resources is your creative potential. You always have the knack of knowing what looks and feels just right. This is as true when it comes to decorating your home as it is regarding matters out there in the big, wide world. If this skill could be allied to confidence on a regular basis, there would be little or nothing to stop you. You may well possess specific skills which others definitely don't have, and you get on best when these are really needed.

Taureans don't mind dealing with routine matters and you have a good administrative ability in a number of different fields. With a deeply intuitive streak (when you are willing to recognise it), it isn't usually hard for you to work out how any particular individual would react under given circumstances. Where you fall down on occasions is that you don't always recognise the great advantages that are yours for the taking, and self-belief could hardly be considered the Taurean's greatest virtue.

Taurus people are good at making lists, even if these are of the mental variety. Your natural warmth makes it possible for you to find friends where others would not, and the sort of advice that you offer is considered and sensible. People feel they can rely on you, a fact that could prove to be one of the most important of your resources. There is nothing at all wrong with using this ability to feather your own nest, particularly since you are not the sort of person who would willingly stand on those around you in order to get where you want to go.

Beneath the surface

To say that you are deep would be a definite understatement. Only you know how far down into the basement some of your considerations and emotions actually go. Because you exhibit a generally practical face to the world at large the true scope of the Taurean mind remains something of a mystery to those around you. Certainly you seem to be uncomplicated and even a little superficial at times, though nothing could be further from the truth. Very little happens to you that fails to be filed away in some recess or other of that great interior that is your mind's library. It may be because of this that Taurus is well known for being able to bear a grudge for a long time. However, what is sometimes forgotten is that you never let a kindness from someone else go without reward, even though it may take you a very long time to find a way to say thank you.

Affairs of the heart are of special importance to you and ties of the romantic kind go as deep as any emotion. Once you love you tend to do so quite unconditionally. It takes months or years of upsets to shake your faith in love, and it's a fact that even in these days of marital splits, Taureans are far more likely than most signs of the zodiac to remain hitched. The simple fact is that you believe in loyalty, absolutely and irrevocably. The thought of letting anyone down once you have given your word is almost unthinkable and if such a situation does occur there are almost always quite definite mitigating factors.

Rules and regulations are easy for you to deal with because you have a natural tendency to order. You are also fairly good at dealing with routines and probably have your own life well sorted out as a result. A word of caution is necessary only when this internal need for order extends too much into your external life. Taureans can be fanatical about having a tidy house or for making things work out exactly as they would wish in a work sense. These tendencies start within the recesses of your own, often closed, mind. The way forward here is to throw open the doors and windows now and again and to let those around you know how you function internally. It isn't easy, because you are quite a closed book at heart. However the exercise is well worthwhile and the results can be quite breathtaking.

Making the best of yourself

Anyone who wants to work to the best of their ability first needs a good deal of self-knowledge. In your case this means recognising just what you are capable of doing and then concentrating in these directions. Of course it's only human nature to be all the things we are not, but this tendency runs deeper in you than it does in the majority of individuals. Use your natural kindness to the full and ally this to your practical ability to get things done. Sorting things out is easy for you, so easy in fact that you sometimes fail to realise that not everyone has these skills to the same extent.

Confidence definitely seems to be evident in the way you deal with the world at large. Of course you know that this often isn't the case, but that doesn't matter. It's the way the world at large views you that counts, so keep moving forward, even on those occasions when you are shaking inside. Use your naturally creative skills to the full and cultivate that innate sense of order in ways that benefit you and the world at a very practical level.

Avoid the tendency to be stubborn by convincing yourself that so many things 'simply don't matter'. An inability to move, simply because you feel annoyed or aggrieved, is certainly going to be more of a hindrance than a help – though there are occasions when, like all facets of nature, it's essential. Cultivate the more cheerful qualities that are endemic to your nature and be prepared to mix freely with as many different sorts of people as you possibly can. Be willing to take on new responsibilities because the more you are able to do so, the greater is your natural sense of self-worth. Stitching all these qualities together and using them to your own advantage isn't always easy, but pays handsomely in the end.

The impressions you give

This is a very interesting section as far as the sign of Taurus is concerned. The reason is very simply that you fail on so many occasions to betray the sheer depth of your own Earth-sign nature. That doesn't mean to say that you come across badly to others. On the contrary, you are probably a very popular person, except with those people who mistreat or cheat others. You have a great sense of what is right, and don't tend to deviate from a point of view once you've come to terms with it.

The world sees you as capable, cheerful and generally active, though with a tendency to be sluggish and lethargic on occasions. Perhaps Taurus needs to explain itself more because even when you are not at your most vibrant best there are invariably reasons. You can be quite secretive, though only usually about yourself. This can make life with the Taurean something of a guessing game on occasions. Certainly you appear to be much more fixed in your attitude than might often be the case. Why should this be so? It's mainly because you do have extremely definite ideas about specific matters, and since you sometimes display these it's natural that others pigeon-hole you as a very 'definite' sort. Actually this is far from being the whole truth but, once again, if you don't explain yourself, others can be left in the dark.

You almost certainly are not short of friends. People recognise that you are friendly, tolerant and extremely supportive. You give the impression of being very trustworthy and people know that they can rely on you to act in a specific manner. If this appears to make you somewhat predictable it doesn't really matter because you are deeply loved, and that's what counts. One fact is almost certain – the world has a greater regard for you than you have for yourself.

The way forward

The ideal life for the Taurus subject seems to be one that is settled and happy, with not too much upheaval and plenty of order. Whether or not this truly turns out to be the case depends on a number of factors. For starters, even those born under the sign of the Bull have a boredom threshold. This means that having to respond to change and diversity probably does you more good than you might at first think. At the same time you won't know exactly what you are capable of doing unless you really stretch yourself, and that's something that you are not always willing to do.

You do function best from within loving relationships, and although you can be very passionate, once you have given your heart you don't tend to change your mind readily. Personal and domestic contentment are worth a great deal to you because they represent the platform upon which you build the rest of your life. You don't make a good itinerant and probably won't indulge in travel for its own sake. Of course it does you good to get around, since anything that broadens your horizons has got to be an advantage, but you'll probably always maintain a solid home base and relish the prospect of coming back to it as frequently as possible.

Most Taureans are family people. You can be a capable parent, though tend to be a little more authoritarian than some types. Keeping an ordered sort of life is at the base of your psychology, so that even when you are young and less tidy-minded there is always a basic desire for self-discipline. This often extends to your work, where you are extremely capable and can quite easily work under your own supervision. You recognise the beautiful in all spheres of life and tend to gravitate towards clean and sanitary surroundings.

In matters of health you tend to be fairly robust, though you can suffer somewhat with headaches, often brought about as a result of a stiff neck and stress. This latter is what you should avoid as much as possible. Saying what you feel, and listening carefully to the responses, is definitely of great importance. The more you learn, the wiser you become. This makes you the natural resort of others when they need help and advice. If you try not to underestimate your own abilities, you can rise as far in life as the world at large thinks you are capable of doing. At the end of the day it is important to recognise your popularity. In all probability your friends have a much higher opinion of you than the one you cultivate for yourself.

TAURUS ON THE CUSP

Astrological profiles are altered for those people born at either the beginning or the end of a zodiac sign, or, more properly, on the cusps of a sign. In the case of Taurus this would be on the 21st of April and for two or three days after, and similarly at the end of the sign, probably from the 18th to the 21st of May.

The Aries Cusp – 21st April to 24th April

Although you have all the refinement, breeding and creative flair of the true Taurean, you are definitely more of a go-getter. Knowing what you want from life, there is a slight possibility that you might be accused of being bossy and sometimes this slightly hurts your Taurean sensitivity. You have plenty of energy to get through the things that you see as being important but it is quite possible that those around you don't always see things in the same light, and this can be annoying to you. Like the typical Taurean you have great reserves of energy and can work long and hard towards any particular objective although, because Aries is also in attendance, you may push yourself slightly harder than is strictly necessary. Your temper is variable and you may not always display the typical Taurean patience with those around you.

It is possible for Taurus to 'wait in the wings' deliberately and therefore to lose out on some of the most important potential gains as a result. In your case, this is much less likely. You don't worry too much about speaking your mind. You are loving and kind, but even family members know that they will only be able to push you so far. At work, you are capable and have executive ability. Like the Taurean you don't really care for getting your hands dirty, but if needs must you can pitch in with the best of them and enjoy a challenge. You don't worry as much as some of your Taurean friends do, but all the same you regularly expect too much of your nervous system and need frequent periods of rest.

Try not to impose your will on those around you and be content to allow things to happen on their own sometimes. This might not be an easy thing for the Aries-cusp Taurean but it's one of the sure ways to success. Confidence isn't lacking and neither is basic patience, but they do have to be encouraged and nurtured.

The Gemini Cusp – 18th May to 21st May

Oh, what a happy person you are – and how much the world loves you for it! This is definitely the more potentially fortunate of the two Taurean cusps, or at least that is how the majority of the people who know you would view it. The fact is that you are bright and breezy, easygoing and sometimes fickle on occasions, but supporting these trends is a patient, generally contented attitude to life that is both refreshing and inspiring. Getting others on your side is not hard and you have plenty of energy when it is needed the most. All the same you are quite capable of dozing in the sun occasionally and probably put far less stress on your nervous system than either Taurus or Gemini when taken alone.

You don't care too much for routines and you love variety, but yet you retain the creative and artistic qualities that come with the sign of the Bull. You work well and with confidence, but would be very likely to change direction in your career at some stage in your life and are not half so tied to routine as is usually the case for Taurus. With a friendly, and even a passionate, approach to matters of the heart you are an attentive lover and a fond parent. Most people know what you really are because you are only too willing to show them. Working out the true motivations that lurk within your soul is part of your personal search to know 'self' and is important.

All in all, you have exactly what it takes to get on in life and a sense of joy and fun that makes you good to know. Patience balances your need to 'get going', whilst your mischievous streak lightens the load of the sign of Taurus which can, on occasions, take itself rather more seriously than it should.

There are many ways of coping with the requirements of life and, at one time or another, it is likely that you will try them all out. But above and beyond your need to experiment you know what is most important to you and that will always be your ultimate goal. What matters the most is your smile, which is enduring and alluring.

TAURUS AND ITS ASCENDANTS

The nature of every individual on the planet is composed of the rich variety of zodiac signs and planetary positions that were present at the time of their birth. Your Sun sign, which in your case is Taurus, is one of the many factors when it comes to assessing the unique person you are. Probably the most important consideration, other than your Sun sign, is to establish the zodiac sign that was rising over the eastern horizon at the time that you were born. This is your Ascending or Rising sign. Most popular astrology fails to take account of the Ascendant, and yet its importance remains with you from the very moment of your birth, through every day of your life. The Ascendant is evident in the way you approach the world, and so, when meeting a person for the first time, it is this astrological influence that you are most likely to notice first. Our Ascending sign essentially represents what we appear to be, while the Sun sign is what we feel inside ourselves.

The Ascendant also has the potential for modifying our overall nature. For example, if you were born at a time of day when Taurus was passing over the eastern horizon (this would be around the time of dawn) then you would be classed as a double Taurus. As such, you would typify this zodiac sign, both internally and in your dealings with others. However, if your Ascendant sign turned out to be a Fire sign, such as Leo, there would be a profound alteration of nature, away from the expected qualities of Taurus.

One of the reasons why popular astrology often ignores the Ascendant is that it has always been rather difficult to establish. We have found a way to make this possible by devising an easy-to-use table, which you will find on page 157 of this book. Using this, you can establish your Ascendant sign at a glance. You will need to know your rough time of birth, then it is simply a case of following the instructions.

For those readers who have no idea of their time of birth it might be worth allowing a good friend, or perhaps your partner, to read through the section that follows this introduction. Someone who deals with you on a regular basis may easily discover your Ascending sign, even though you could have some difficulty establishing it for yourself. A good understanding of this component of your nature is essential if you want to be aware of that 'other person' who is responsible for the way you make contact with the world at large. Your Sun sign, Ascendant sign, and the other pointers in this book will, together, allow you a far better understanding of what makes you tick as an individual. Peeling back the different layers of your astrological make-up can be an enlightening experience, and the Ascendant may represent one of the most important layers of all.

Taurus with Taurus Ascendant

The world would see you as being fairly typical of the sign of Taurus, so you are careful, sensitive, well mannered and, if other astrological trends agree, very creative. Nothing pleases you more than a tidy environment to live in and a peaceful life. You probably believe that there is a place for everything and will do your best to keep it all where it should be. It's a pity that this sometimes includes people, and you are certain to get rather irritated if they don't behave in the way that you would expect. Despite this, you are generally understanding and are very capable of giving and receiving affection.

Not everyone knows the real you, however, and it is sometimes difficult to tell the world those most personal details that can be locked deep inside. At an emotional level you tend to idealise love somewhat, though if anything this presents itself to the world as a slight 'coldness' on occasions. This is far from the truth, but your tidy mind demands that even the most intimate processes are subjected to the same sense of order with which you view the world at large. Unlike many sign combinations, you don't really rely on the help and support of others because you are more than capable yourself. In the main you live a happy life and have the ability to pass on this trait to those you care for.

Taurus with Gemini Ascendant

This is a generally happy combination which finds you better able to externalise the cultured and creative qualities which are inherent in your Taurean nature. You love to be around interesting and stimulating people and tend to be much more talkative than the typical Taurean is expected to be. The reason why Gemini helps here is because it lightens the load somewhat. Taurus is not the most introspective sign of the zodiac, but it does have that quality, and a good dose of Gemini allows you to speak your mind more freely and, as a result, to know yourself better too.

Although your mind tends to be fairly logical, you also enjoy flashes of insight that can cause you to behave in a less rational way from time to time. This is probably no bad thing because life will never be boring with you around. You try to convince yourself that you take on board all the many and varied opinions that come back at you from others, though there is a slight danger of intellectual snobbery if the responses you get are not the expected ones. You particularly like clean houses, funny people and probably fast cars. Financial rewards can come thick and fast to the Gemini-Ascendant Taurean when the logical but inspirational mind is harnessed to practical matters.

Taurus with Cancer Ascendant

Your main aim in life seems to be to look after everyone and everything that you come across. From your deepest and most enduring human love, right down to the birds in the park, you really do care and you show that natural affection in a thousand different ways. Your nature is sensitive and you are easily moved to tears, though this does not prevent you from pitching in and doing practical things to assist at just about any level. There is a danger that you could stifle those same people whom you set out to assist, and people with this zodiac combination are often unwilling, or unable, to allow their children to grow and leave the nest. More time spent considering what suits you would be no bad thing, but the problem is that you find it almost impossible to imagine any situation that doesn't involve your most basic need, which is to nurture.

You appear not to possess a selfish streak, though it sometimes turns out that, in being certain that you understand the needs and wants of the world, you are nevertheless treading on their toes. This eventual realisation can be very painful, but it isn't a stick with which you should beat yourself because at heart you are one of the kindest people imaginable. Your sense of fair play means that you are a quiet social reformer at heart.

Taurus with Leo Ascendant

Oh dear, this can be rather a hedonistic combination. The trouble is that Taurus tends to have a great sense of what looks and feels right, whilst Leo, being a Cat, is inclined to preen itself on almost any occasion. The combination tends towards self-love, which is all too likely for someone who is perfect. But don't be too dispirited about these facts because there is a great deal going for you in other ways. For a start you have one of the warmest hearts to be found anywhere and you are so brave that others marvel at the courage you display. The mountains that you climb may not be of the large, rocky sort, but you manage to find plenty of pinnacles to scale all the same, and you invariably get to the top.

Routines might bore you a little more than would be the case with Taurus alone, but you don't mind being alone. Why should you? You are probably the nicest person you know! Thus if you were ever to be cast up on a deserted island you would people the place all on your own, and there would never be any crime, untidiness or arguments. Problems only arise when other people are involved. However, in social settings you are charming, good to know and full of ideas that really have legs. You preserve your youth well into middle age, but at base you can tend to worry more than is good for you.

Taurus with Virgo Ascendant

This combination tends to amplify the Taurean qualities that you naturally possess and this is the case because both Taurus and Virgo are Earth signs. However, there are certain factors related to Virgo that show themselves very differently than the sign's cousin, Taurus. Virgo is more fussy, nervy and pedantic than Taurus and all of these qualities are going to show up in your nature at one level or another. On the plus side, you might be slightly less concerned about having a perfect home and a perfect family, and your interest in life appears at a more direct level than that of the true Taurean. You care very much about your home and family and are very loyal to your friends. It's true that you sometimes try and take them over, and you can also show a marked tendency to dominate, but your heart is in the right place, and most people recognise that your caring is genuine.

One problem is that there are very few shades of grey in your life, which is certainly not the case for other zodiac sign combinations. Living your life in the way that you do, there isn't much room for compromise, and this fact alone can prove to be something of a problem where relationships are concerned. In a personal sense you need a partner who is willing to be organised and one who relies heavily on your judgements, which don't change very often.

Taurus with Libra Ascendant

A fortunate combination in many ways, this is a double Venus rulership, since both Taurus and Libra are heavily reliant on the planet of love. You are social, amiable and a natural diplomat, anxious to please and ready to care for just about anyone who shows interest in you. You hate disorder, which means that there is a place for everything and everything in its place. This can throw up the odd paradox, however, since being half Libran you cannot always work out where that place ought to be! You deal with life in a humorous way and are quite capable of seeing the absurd in yourself, as well as in others. Your heart is no bigger than that of the dyed-in-the-wool Taurean, but it sits rather closer to the surface and so others recognise it more.

On those occasions when you know you are standing on firm ground you can show great confidence, even if you have to be ready to change some of your opinions at the drop of a hat. When this happens you can be quite at odds with yourself, because Taurus doesn't take very many U-turns, whereas Libra does. Don't expect to know yourself too well, and keep looking for the funny side of things, because it is within humour that you forge the sort of life that suits you best.

Taurus with Scorpio Ascendant

The first, last and most important piece of advice for you is not to take yourself, or anyone else, too seriously. This might be rather a tall order because Scorpio intensifies the deeper qualities of Taurus and can make you rather lacking in the sense of humour that we all need to live our lives in this most imperfect of worlds. You are naturally sensuous by nature. This shows itself in a host of ways. In all probability you can spend hours in the bath, love to treat yourself to good food and drink and take your greatest pleasure in neat and orderly surroundings. On occasions this can alienate you from those who live in the same house, because other people do need to use the bathroom from time to time, and they cannot remain tidy indefinitely.

You tend to worry a great deal about things which are really not very important, but don't take this statement too seriously or you will begin to worry about this, too! You often need to lighten up and should always do your best to tell yourself that most things are not half so important as they seem to be. Be careful over the selection of a life partner and if possible choose someone who is naturally funny and who does not take life anywhere near as seriously as you are inclined to do. At work you are more than capable and in all probability everyone relies heavily on your wise judgements.

Taurus with Sagittarius Ascendant

A dual nature is evident here, and if it doesn't serve to confuse you, it will certainly be a cause of concern to many of the people with whom you share your life. You like to have a good time and are a natural party-goer. On such occasions you are accommodating, chatty and good to know. But contrast this with the quieter side of Taurus, which is directly opposed to your Sagittarian qualities. The opposition of forces is easy for you to deal with because you inhabit your own body and mind all the time, but it's far less easy for friends and relatives to understand. So on those occasions when you decide that, socially speaking, enough is enough, you may have trouble explaining this to the twelve people who are waiting outside your door with party hats and whoopee cushions.

Confidence to do almost anything is not far from the forefront of your mind and you readily embark on adventures that would have some types flapping about in horror. Here again, it is important to realise that we are not all built the same way and that gentle coaxing is sometimes necessary to bring others round to your point of view. If you really have a fault it could be that you are so busy being your own, rather less than predictable self, that you fail to take the rest of the world into account.

Taurus with Capricorn Ascendant

It might appear on the surface that you are not the most interesting person in the world. This is a pity, for you have an active though very logical mind, so logical in some instances that you would have a great deal in common with Mr Spock. This is the thorn in your flesh, or rather the flesh of everyone else, since you are probably quite happy being exactly what you are. You can think things through in a clear and very practical way and end up taking decisions that are balanced, eminently sensible, but, on occasions, rather dull.

Actually there is a fun machine somewhere deep within that Earth-sign nature and those who know you the best will recognise the fact. Often this combination is attended by a deep and biting sense of humour, but it's of the sort that less intelligent and considered types would find rather difficult to recognise. It is likely that you have no lack of confidence in your own judgement and you have all the attributes necessary to do very well on the financial front. Slow and steady progress is your way and you need to be quite certain before you commit yourself to any new venture. This is a zodiac combination that can soak up years of stress and numerous difficulties, yet still come out on top. Nothing holds you back for long and you tend to be very brave.

Taurus with Aquarius Ascendant

There is nothing that you fail to think about deeply and with great intensity. You are wise, honest and very scientific in your approach to life. Routines are necessary in life, but you have most of them sorted out well in advance and so always have time to look at the next interesting fact. If you don't spend all your time watching documentaries on television, you make a good friend and love to socialise. Most of the great discoveries of the world were probably made by people with this sort of astrological combination, though your nature is rather 'odd' on occasions and so can be difficult for others to understand.

You may be most surprised when others tell you that you are eccentric, but you don't really mind too much because for half of the time you are not inhabiting the same world as the rest of us. Because you can be delightfully dotty you are probably much loved and cherished by your friends, of which there are likely to be many. Family members probably adore you too and you can be guaranteed to entertain anyone with whom you come into contact. The only fly in the ointment is that you sometimes lose track of reality, and fly high in your own atmosphere of rarefied possibilities.

Taurus with Pisces Ascendant

You are clearly a very sensitive type of person and that sometimes makes it rather difficult for others to know how they might best approach you. Private and deep, you are nevertheless socially inclined on many occasions. However, because your nature is bottomless it is possible that some types would actually accuse you of being shallow. How can this come about? Well, it's simple really. The fact is that you rarely show anyone what is going on in the deepest recesses of your mind and so your responses can appear to be trite or even ill-considered. This is far from the truth, as those who are allowed into the 'inner sanctum' would readily admit. You are something of a sensualist, and relish staying in bed late and simply pleasing yourself for days on end. However, you are a Taurean at heart so you desire a tidy environment in which to live your usually long life.

You are able to deal with the routine aspects of life quite well and can be a capable worker once you are up and firing on all cylinders. It is very important that you maintain an interest in what you are doing because the recesses of your dreamy mind can sometimes appear to be infinitely more attractive. Your imagination is second to none and this fact can often be turned to your advantage.

Taurus with Aries Ascendant

This is a steady combination, so much so that even experienced astrologers would be unlikely to recognise that the Aries quality is present at all, unless of course they came to know you very well. Your approach to life tends to be slow and considered and there is a great danger that you could suppress those feelings that others of your kind would be only too willing to verbalise. To compensate, you are deeply creative and will think matters through much more readily than more dominant Aries types would be inclined to do. In your dealings with the world, you are, nevertheless, somewhat locked inside yourself and can struggle to achieve the level of communication that you so desperately need. Frustration might follow, were it not for the fact that you possess a quiet determination that, to those in the know, is the clearest window through to your Taurean soul.

The care for others is strong and you certainly demonstrate this at all levels. The fact is that you live a great percentage of your life in service to the people you take to, whilst at the same time being able to shut the door firmly in the face of people who irritate or anger you. You are deeply motivated towards family relationships.

THE MOON AND THE PART IT PLAYS IN YOUR LIFE

In astrology the Moon is probably the single most important heavenly body after the Sun. Its unique position, as partner to the Earth on its journey around the solar system, means that the Moon appears to pass through the signs of the zodiac extremely quickly. The zodiac position of the Moon at the time of your birth plays a great part in personal character and is especially significant in the build-up of your emotional nature.

Your Own Moon Sign

Discovering the position of the Moon at the time of your birth has always been notoriously difficult because tracking the complex zodiac positions of the Moon is not easy. This process has been reduced to three simple stages with our Lunar Tables. A breakdown of the Moon's zodiac positions can be found from page 35 onwards, so that once you know what your Moon Sign is, you can see what part this plays in the overall build-up of your personal character.

If you follow the instructions on the next page you will soon be able to work out exactly what zodiac sign the Moon occupied on the day that you were born and you can then go on to compare the reading for this position with those of your Sun sign and your Ascendant. It is partly the comparison between these three important positions that goes towards making you the unique individual you are.

How To Discover Your Moon Sign

This is a three-stage process. You may need a pen and a piece of paper but if you follow the instructions below the process should only take a minute or so.

STAGE 1 First of all you need to know the Moon Age at the time of your birth. If you look at Moon Table 1, on page 33, you will find all the years between 1921 and 2019 down the left side. Find the year of your birth and then trace across to the right to the month of your birth. Where the two intersect you will find a number. This is the date of the New Moon in the month that you were born. You now need to count forward the number of days between the New Moon and your own birthday. For example, if the New Moon in the month of your birth was shown as being the 6th and you were born on the 20th, your Moon Age Day would be 14. If the New Moon in the month of your birth came after your birthday, you need to count forward from the New Moon in the previous month. Whatever the result, jot this number down so that you do not forget it.

STAGE 2 Take a look at Moon Table 2 on page 34. Down the left hand column look for the date of your birth. Now trace across to the month of your birth. Where the two meet you will find a letter. Copy this letter down alongside your Moon Age Day.

STAGE 3 Moon Table 3 on page 34 will supply you with the zodiac sign the Moon occupied on the day of your birth. Look for your Moon Age Day down the left hand column and then for the letter you found in Stage 2. Where the two converge you will find a zodiac sign and this is the sign occupied by the Moon on the day that you were born.

Your Zodiac Moon Sign Explained

You will find a profile of all zodiac Moon Signs on pages 35 to 38, showing in yet another way how astrology helps to make you into the individual that you are. In each daily entry of the Astral Diary you can find the zodiac position of the Moon for every day of the year. This also allows you to discover your lunar birthdays. Since the Moon passes through all the signs of the zodiac in about a month, you can expect something like twelve lunar birthdays each year. At these times you are likely to be emotionally steady and able to make the sort of decisions that have real, lasting value.

MOON TABLE 1

YEAR	MAR	APR	MAY	YEAR	MAR	APR	MAY	YEAR	MAR	APR	MAY
1921	9	8	7	1954	5	3	2	1987	29	28	27
1922	28	27	26	1955	24	22	21	1988	18	16	15
1923	17	16	15	1956	12	11	10	1989	7	6	5
1924	5	4	3	1957	1/31	29	29	1990	26	25	24
1925	24	23	22	1958	20	19	18	1991	15	13	13
1926	14	12	11	1959	9	8	7	1992	4	3	2
1927	3	2	1/30	1960	27	26	26	1993	24	22	21
1928	21	20	19	1961	16	15	14	1994	12	11	10
1929	11	9	9	1962	6	5	4	1995	30	29	29
1930	30	28	28	1963	25	23	23	1996	19	18	18
1931	19	18	17	1964	14	12	11	1997	9	7	6
1932	7	6	5	1965	2	1	1/30	1998	27	26	25
1933	26	24	24	1966	21	20	19	1999	17	16	15
1934	15	13	13	1967	10	9	8	2000	6	4	4
1935	5	3	2	1968	29	28	27	2001	24	23	22
1936	23	21	20	1969	18	16	15	2002	13	12	10
1937	13	12	10	1970	7	6	6	2003	2	1	1/30
1938	2/31	30	29	1971	26	25	24	2004	21	19	18
1939	20	19	19	1972	15	13	13	2005	10	8	8
1940	9	7	7	1973	5	3	2	2006	29	27	27
1941	27	26	26	1974	24	22	21	2007	18	17	15
1942	16	15	15	1975	12	11	11	2008	7	6	5
1943	6	4	4	1976	30	29	29	2009	26	25	24
1944	24	22	22	1977	19	18	18	2010	15	14	14
1945	14	12	11	1978	9	7	7	2011	5	3	3
1946	3	2	1/30	1979	27	26	26	2012	22	21	20
1947	21	20	19	1980	16	15	14	2013	12	10	10
1948	11	9	9	1981	6	4	4	2014	1/31	30	29
1949	29	28	27	1982	24	23	21	2015	20	19	18
1950	18	17	17	1983	14	13	12	2016	8	7	8
1951	7	6	6	1984	2	1	1/30	2017	27	25	25
1952	25	24	23	1985	21	20	19	2018	17	16	15
1953	15	13	13	1986	10	9	8	2019	5	4	3

TABLE 2

DAY	APR	MAY
1	J	M
2	J	M
3	J	M
4	J	M
5	J	M
6	J	M
7	J	M
8	J	M
9	J	M
10	J	M
11	K	M
12	K	N
13	K	N
14	K	N
15	K	N
16	K	N
17	K	N
18	K	N
19	K	N
20	K	N
21	L	N
22	L	O
23	L	O
24	L	O
25	L	O
26	L	O
27	L	O
28	L	O
29	L	O
30	L	O
31	–	O

MOON TABLE 3

M/D	J	K	L	M	N	O	P
0	AR	TA	TA	TA	GE	GE	GE
1	TA	TA	TA	GE	GE	GE	CA
2	TA	TA	GE	GE	GE	CA	CA
3	TA	GE	GE	GE	CA	CA	CA
4	GE	GE	GE	CA	CA	CA	LE
5	GE	CA	CA	CA	LE	LE	LE
6	CA	CA	CA	LE	LE	LE	VI
7	CA	CA	LE	LE	LE	VI	VI
8	CA	LE	LE	LE	VI	VI	VI
9	LE	LE	VI	VI	VI	LI	LI
10	LE	VI	VI	VI	LI	LI	LI
11	VI	VI	VI	LI	LI	SC	SC
12	VI	VI	LI	LI	LI	SC	SC
13	VI	LI	LI	LI	SC	SC	SC
14	LI	LI	LI	SC	SC	SA	SA
15	LI	SC	SC	SC	SA	SA	SA
16	SC	SC	SC	SA	SA	SA	CP
17	SC	SC	SA	SA	SA	CP	CP
18	SC	SA	SA	SA	CP	CP	CP
19	SA	SA	SA	CP	CP	CP	AQ
20	SA	CP	CP	CP	AQ	AQ	AQ
21	CP	CP	CP	AQ	AQ	AQ	PI
22	CP	CP	AQ	AQ	AQ	PI	PI
23	CP	AQ	AQ	AQ	PI	PI	PI
24	AQ	AQ	AQ	PI	PI	PI	AR
25	AQ	PI	PI	PI	AR	AR	AR
26	PI	PI	PI	AR	AR	AR	TA
27	PI	PI	AR	AR	AR	TA	TA
28	PI	AR	AR	AR	TA	TA	TA
29	AR	AR	AR	TA	TA	TA	GE

AR = Aries, TA = Taurus, GE = Gemini, CA = Cancer, LE = Leo, VI = Virgo,
LI = Libra, SC = Scorpio, SA = Sagittarius, CP = Capricorn, AQ = Aquarius, PI = Pisces

MOON SIGNS

Moon in Aries

You have a strong imagination, courage, determination and a desire to do things in your own way and forge your own path through life.

Originality is a key attribute; you are seldom stuck for ideas although your mind is changeable and you could take the time to focus on individual tasks. Often quick-tempered, you take orders from few people and live life at a fast pace. Avoid health problems by taking regular time out for rest and relaxation.

Emotionally, it is important that you talk to those you are closest to and work out your true feelings. Once you discover that people are there to help, there is less necessity for you to do everything yourself.

Moon in Taurus

The Moon in Taurus gives you a courteous and friendly manner, which means you are likely to have many friends.

The good things in life mean a lot to you, as Taurus is an Earth sign that delights in experiences which please the senses. Hence you are probably a lover of good food and drink, which may in turn mean you need to keep an eye on the bathroom scales, especially as looking good is also important to you.

Emotionally you are fairly stable and you stick by your own standards. Taureans do not respond well to change. Intuition also plays an important part in your life.

Moon in Gemini

You have a warm-hearted character, sympathetic and eager to help others. At times reserved, you can also be articulate and chatty: this is part of the paradox of Gemini, which always brings duplicity to the nature. You are interested in current affairs, have a good intellect, are good company and likely to have many friends. Most of your friends have a high opinion of you and would be ready to defend you should the need arise. However, this is usually unnecessary, as you are quite capable of defending yourself in any verbal confrontation.

Travel is important to your inquisitive mind and you find intellectual stimulus in mixing with people from different cultures. You also gain much from reading, writing and the arts but you do need plenty of rest and relaxation in order to avoid fatigue.

Moon in Cancer

The Moon in Cancer at the time of birth is a fortunate position as Cancer is the Moon's natural home. This means that the qualities of compassion and understanding given by the Moon are especially enhanced in your nature, and you are friendly and sociable and cope well with emotional pressures. You cherish home and family life, and happily do the domestic tasks. Your surroundings are important to you and you hate squalor and filth. You are likely to have a love of music and poetry.

Your basic character, although at times changeable like the Moon itself, depends on symmetry. You aim to make your surroundings comfortable and harmonious, for yourself and those close to you.

Moon in Leo

The best qualities of the Moon and Leo come together to make you warm-hearted, fair, ambitious and self-confident. With good organisational abilities, you invariably rise to a position of responsibility in your chosen career. This is fortunate as you don't enjoy being an 'also-ran' and would rather be an important part of a small organisation than a menial in a large one.

You should be lucky in love, and happy, provided you put in the effort to make a comfortable home for yourself and those close to you. It is likely that you will have a love of pleasure, sport, music and literature. Life brings you many rewards, most of them as a direct result of your own efforts, although you may be luckier than average and ready to make the best of any situation.

Moon in Virgo

You are endowed with good mental abilities and a keen receptive memory, but you are never ostentatious or pretentious. Naturally quite reserved, you still have many friends, especially of the opposite sex. Marital relationships must be discussed carefully and worked at so that they remain harmonious, as personal attachments can be a problem if you do not give them your full attention.

Talented and persevering, you possess artistic qualities and are a good homemaker. Earning your honours through genuine merit, you work long and hard towards your objectives but show little pride in your achievements. Many short journeys will be undertaken in your life.

Moon in Libra

With the Moon in Libra you are naturally popular and make friends easily. People like you, probably more than you realise, you bring fun to a party and are a natural diplomat. For all its good points, Libra is not the most stable of astrological signs and, as a result, your emotions can be a little unstable too. Therefore, although the Moon in Libra is said to be good for love and marriage, your Sun sign and Rising sign will have an important effect on your emotional and loving qualities.

You must remember to relate to others in your decision-making. Co-operation is crucial because Libra represents the 'balance' of life that can only be achieved through harmonious relationships. Conformity is not easy for you because Libra, an Air sign, likes its independence.

Moon in Scorpio

Some people might call you pushy. In fact, all you really want to do is to live life to the full and protect yourself and your family from the pressures of life. Take care to avoid giving the impression of being sarcastic or impulsive and use your energies wisely and constructively.

You have great courage and you invariably achieve your goals by force of personality and sheer effort. You are fond of mystery and are good at predicting the outcome of situations and events. Travel experiences can be beneficial to you.

You may experience problems if you do not take time to examine your motives in a relationship, and also if you allow jealousy, always a feature of Scorpio, to cloud your judgement.

Moon in Sagittarius

The Moon in Sagittarius helps to make you a generous individual with humanitarian qualities and a kind heart. Restlessness may be intrinsic as your mind is seldom still. Perhaps because of this, you have a need for change that could lead you to several major moves during your adult life. You are not afraid to stand your ground when you know your judgement is right, you speak directly and have good intuition.

At work you are quick, efficient and versatile and so you make an ideal employee. You need work to be intellectually demanding and do not enjoy tedious routines.

In relationships, you anger quickly if faced with stupidity or deception, though you are just as quick to forgive and forget. Emotionally, there are times when your heart rules your head.

Moon in Capricorn

The Moon in Capricorn makes you popular and likely to come into the public eye in some way. The watery Moon is not entirely comfortable in the Earth sign of Capricorn and this may lead to some difficulties in the early years of life. An initial lack of creative ability and indecision must be overcome before the true qualities of patience and perseverance inherent in Capricorn can show through.

You have good administrative ability and are a capable worker, and if you are careful you can accumulate wealth. But you must be cautious and take professional advice in partnerships, as you are open to deception. You may be interested in social or welfare work, which suit your organisational skills and sympathy for others.

Moon in Aquarius

The Moon in Aquarius makes you an active and agreeable person with a friendly, easy-going nature. Sympathetic to the needs of others, you flourish in a laid-back atmosphere. You are broad-minded, fair and open to suggestion, although sometimes you have an unconventional quality which others can find hard to understand.

You are interested in the strange and curious, and in old articles and places. You enjoy trips to these places and gain much from them. Political, scientific and educational work interests you and you might choose a career in science or technology.

Money-wise, you make gains through innovation and concentration and Lunar Aquarians often tackle more than one job at a time. In love you are kind and honest.

Moon in Pisces

You have a kind, sympathetic nature, somewhat retiring at times, but you always take account of others' feelings and help when you can.

Personal relationships may be problematic, but as life goes on you can learn from your experiences and develop a better understanding of yourself and the world around you.

You have a fondness for travel, appreciate beauty and harmony and hate disorder and strife. You may be fond of literature and would make a good writer or speaker yourself. You have a creative imagination and may come across as an incurable romantic. You have strong intuition, maybe bordering on a mediumistic quality, which sets you apart from the mass. You may not be rich in cash terms, but your personal gifts are worth more than gold.

TAURUS IN LOVE

Discover how compatible in love you are with people from the same and other signs of the zodiac. Five stars equals a match made in heaven!

Taurus meets Taurus

A certainty for complete success or absolute failure. Taurus has enough self-knowledge to recognise the strengths of a fellow Taurean, so these two can live in harmony. Both will be tidy and live in comfortable surroundings. Two Taureans seldom argue and will be good friends. But something may be lacking – a spark that doesn't ignite. Passion is important and Taurus reflects, rather than creates it. The prognosis is good, but someone must turn the heat up to get things really cooking. Star rating: ****

Taurus meets Gemini

Gemini people can infuriate the generally steady Taurean nature as they are so untidy, which is a complete reversal of the Taurean ethos. At first this won't matter; Mr or Miss Gemini is enchanting, entertaining and very different. But time will tell, and that's why this potential relationship only has two stars. There is hope, however, because Taurus can curb some of the excesses of the Twins, whilst Gemini is capable of preventing the Bull from taking itself too seriously. Star rating: **

Taurus meets Cancer

This pair will have the tidiest house in the street – every stick of furniture in place, and no errant blade of grass daring to spoil the lawn. But things inside the relationship might not be quite so ship-shape as both signs need, but don't offer, encouragement. There's plenty of affection, but few incentives for mutual progress. This might not prevent material success, but an enduring relationship isn't based on money alone. Passion is essential, and both parties need to realise and aim for that. Star rating: **

Taurus meets Leo

Here we find a generally successful pairing, which frequently leads to an enduring relationship. Taurus needs stimulation which Leo is happy to offer, while Leo responds well to the Bull's sense of order. The essence of the relationship is balance, but it may be achieved with wild swings of the scales on the way, so don't expect a quiet life, though this pair will enjoy a reconciliation after an argument! Material success is probable and, as both like children, a family is likely. Star rating: ***

Taurus meets Virgo

This is a difficult basis for a successful relationship, and yet it often works. Both signs are from the Earth element, so have a common-sense approach to life. They have a mutual understanding, and share many interests. Taurus understands and copes well with Virgo's fussy nature, while Virgo revels in the Bull's tidy and artistic qualities. Both sides are committed to achieving lasting material success. There won't be fireworks, and the match may lack a certain 'spiritual' feel, but as that works both ways it may not be a problem. Star rating: *****

Taurus meets Libra

A happy life is important to both these signs and, as they are both ruled by Venus, they share a common understanding, even though they display themselves so differently. Taurus is quieter than Libra, but can be decisive, and that's what counts. Libra is interested in absolutely everything, an infectious quality when seen through Taurean eyes. The slightly flighty qualities of Libra may lead to jealousy from the Bull. Not an argumentative relationship and one that often works well. There could be many changes of address for this pair. Star rating: ****

Taurus meets Scorpio

Scorpio is deep – very deep – which may be a problem, because Taurus doesn't wear its heart on its sleeve either. It might be difficult for this pair to get together, because neither are naturally inclined to make the first move. Taurus stands in awe of the power and intensity of the Scorpio mind, while the Scorpion is interested in the Bull's affable and friendly qualities, so an enduring relationship could be forged if the couple ever get round to talking. Both are lovers of home and family, which will help to cement a relationship. Star rating: **

Taurus meets Sagittarius

On first impression, Taurus may not like Sagittarius, who may seem brash, and even common, when viewed through the Bull's refined eyes. But there is hope of success because the two signs have so much to offer each other. The Archer is enthralled by the Taurean's natural poise and beauty, while Taurus always needs more basic confidence, which is no problem to Sagittarius who has plenty to spare. Both signs love to travel. There are certain to be ups and downs, but that doesn't prevent an interesting, inspiring and even exciting combination. Star rating: ***

Taurus meets Capricorn

If not quite a match made in heaven, this comes close. Both signs are earthy in nature and that is a promising start. Capricorn is very practical and can make a Taurean's dreams come true. Both are tidy, like to know what is going to happen in a day-to-day sense, and are steady and committed. Taurus loves refinement, which Capricorn accepts and even helps to create. A good prognosis for material success rounds off a relationship that could easily stay the course. The only thing missing is a genuine sense of humour. Star rating: *****

Taurus meets Aquarius

In any relationship of which Aquarius is a part, surprises abound. It is difficult for Taurus to understand the soul-searching, adventurous, changeable Aquarian, but on the positive side, the Bull is adaptable and can respond well to a dose of excitement. Aquarians are kind and react well to the same quality coming back at them. Both are friendly, capable of deep affection and basically quite creative. Unfortunately, though, Taurus simply doesn't know what makes Aquarius tick, which could lead to hidden feelings of isolation. Star rating: **

Taurus meets Pisces

No problem here, unless both parties come from the quieter side of their respective signs. Most of the time Taurus and Pisces would live comfortably together, offering mutual support and deep regard. Taurus can offer the personal qualities that Pisces craves, whilst Pisces understands and copes with the Bull's slightly stubborn qualities. Taurus is likely to travel in Piscean company, so there is a potential for wide-ranging experiences and variety which is essential. There will be some misunderstandings, mainly because Pisces is so deep, but that won't prevent their enduring happiness. Star rating: ***

Taurus meets Aries

This match has been known to work very well. Aries brings dynamism and ambition, while Taurus has the patience to see things through logically. Such complementary views work equally well in a relationship or in an office environment. There is mutual respect, but sometimes a lack of total understanding. The romantic needs of each sign are quite different, but both are still fulfilled. Taurus and Aries can live easily in domestic harmony which is very important but, interestingly, Aries may be the loser in battles of will. Star rating: ***

VENUS:
THE PLANET OF LOVE

If you look up at the sky around sunset or sunrise you will often see Venus in close attendance to the Sun. It is arguably one of the most beautiful sights of all and there is little wonder that historically it became associated with the goddess of love. But although Venus does play an important part in the way you view love and in the way others see you romantically, this is only one of the spheres of influence that it enjoys in your overall character.

Venus has a part to play in the more cultured side of your life and has much to do with your appreciation of art, literature, music and general creativity. Even the way you look is responsive to the part of the zodiac that Venus occupied at the start of your life, though this fact is also down to your Sun sign and Ascending sign. If, at the time you were born, Venus occupied one of the more gregarious zodiac signs, you will be more likely to wear your heart on your sleeve, as well as to be more attracted to entertainment, social gatherings and good company. If on the other hand Venus occupied a quiet zodiac sign at the time of your birth, you would tend to be more retiring and less willing to shine in public situations.

It's good to know what part the planet Venus plays in your life, for it can have a great bearing on the way you appear to the rest of the world and since we all have to mix with others, you can learn to make the very best of what Venus has to offer you.

One of the great complications in the past has always been trying to establish exactly what zodiac position Venus enjoyed when you were born, because the planet is notoriously difficult to track. However, we have solved that problem by creating a table that is exclusive to your Sun sign, which you will find on the following page.

Establishing your Venus sign could not be easier. Just look up the year of your birth on the following page and you will see a sign of the zodiac. This was the sign that Venus occupied in the period covered by your sign in that year. If Venus occupied more than one sign during the period, this is indicated by the date on which the sign changed, and the name of the new sign. For instance, if you were born in 1950, Venus was in Pisces until the 5th May, after which time it was in Aries. If you were born before 5th May your Venus sign is Pisces, if you were born on or after 5th May, your Venus sign is Aries. Once you have established the position of Venus at the time of your birth, you can then look in the pages which follow to see how this has a bearing on your life as a whole.

1921 TAURUS / 27.4 ARIES
1922 TAURUS / 2.5 GEMINI
1923 PISCES / 27.4 ARIES
1924 GEMINI / 7.5 CANCER
1925 TAURUS / 16.5 GEMINI
1926 PISCES / 6.5 ARIES
1927 GEMINI / 12.5 CANCER
1928 ARIES / 6.5 TAURUS
1929 TAURUS / 24.4 ARIES
1930 TAURUS / 1.5 GEMINI
1931 PISCES / 26.4 ARIES
1932 GEMINI / 8.5 CANCER
1933 TAURUS / 15.5 GEMINI
1934 PISCES / 6.5 ARIES
1935 GEMINI / 12.5 CANCER
1936 ARIES / 6.5 TAURUS
1937 TAURUS / 21.4 ARIES
1938 TAURUS / 1.5 GEMINI
1939 PISCES / 26.4 ARIES
1940 GEMINI / 9.5 CANCER
1941 TAURUS / 14.5 GEMINI
1942 PISCES / 6.5 ARIES
1943 GEMINI / 11.5 CANCER
1944 ARIES / 6.5 TAURUS
1945 ARIES
1946 TAURUS / 30.4 GEMINI
1947 PISCES / 25.4 ARIES
1948 GEMINI / 9.5 CANCER
1949 TAURUS / 14.5 GEMINI
1950 PISCES / 5.5 ARIES
1951 GEMINI / 11.5 CANCER
1952 ARIES / 5.5 TAURUS
1953 ARIES
1954 TAURUS / 29.4 GEMINI
1955 PISCES / 25.4 ARIES
1956 GEMINI / 10.5 CANCER
1957 TAURUS / 13.5 GEMINI
1958 PISCES / 5.5 ARIES
1959 GEMINI / 10.5 CANCER
1960 ARIES / 4.5 TAURUS
1961 ARIES
1962 TAURUS / 28.4 GEMINI
1963 PISCES / 24.4 ARIES
1964 GEMINI / 11.5 CANCER
1965 TAURUS / 13.5 GEMINI
1966 PISCES / 5.5 ARIES
1967 GEMINI / 10.5 CANCER
1968 ARIES / 4.5 TAURUS
1969 ARIES
1970 TAURUS / 27.4 GEMINI

1971 PISCES / 24.4 ARIES
1972 GEMINI / 12.5 CANCER
1973 TAURUS / 12.5 GEMINI
1974 PISCES / 4.5 ARIES
1975 GEMINI / 9.5 CANCER
1976 ARIES / 3.5 TAURUS
1977 ARIES
1978 TAURUS / 27.4 GEMINI
1979 PISCES / 23.4 ARIES
1980 GEMINI / 13.5 CANCER
1981 TAURUS / 12.5 GEMINI
1982 PISCES / 4.5 ARIES
1983 GEMINI / 9.5 CANCER
1984 ARIES / 3.5 TAURUS
1985 ARIES
1986 TAURUS / 26.4 GEMINI
1987 PISCES / 23.4 ARIES
1988 GEMINI / 15.5 CANCER
1989 TAURUS / 11.5 GEMINI
1990 PISCES / 4.5 ARIES
1991 GEMINI / 8.5 CANCER
1992 ARIES / 2.5 TAURUS
1993 ARIES
1994 TAURUS / 26.4 GEMINI
1995 PISCES / 22.4 ARIES
1996 GEMINI / 15.5 CANCER
1997 TAURUS / 11.5 GEMINI
1998 PISCES / 3.5 ARIES
1999 GEMINI / 8.5 CANCER
2000 ARIES / 2.5 TAURUS
2001 ARIES
2002 TAURUS / 26.4 GEMINI
2003 PISCES / 22.4 ARIES
2004 GEMINI / 15.5 CANCER
2005 TAURUS / 11.5 GEMINI
2006 PISCES / 3.5 ARIES
2007 GEMINI / 8.5 CANCER
2008 ARIES / 2.5 TAURUS
2009 ARIES
2010 TAURUS / 26.4 GEMINI
2011 PISCES / 22.4 ARIES
2012 PISCES / 22.4 ARIES
2013 PISCES / 3.5 ARIES
2014 PISCES / 3.5 ARIES
2015 GEMINI / 8.5 CANCER
2016 TAURUS
2017 GEMINI / 15.5 CANCER
2018 TAURUS / 26.4 GEMINI
2019 PISCES / 22.4 ARIES

VENUS THROUGH THE ZODIAC SIGNS

Venus in Aries

Amongst other things, the position of Venus in Aries indicates a fondness for travel, music and all creative pursuits. Your nature tends to be affectionate and you would try not to create confusion or difficulty for others if it could be avoided. Many people with this planetary position have a great love of the theatre, and mental stimulation is of the greatest importance. Early romantic attachments are common with Venus in Aries, so it is very important to establish a genuine sense of romantic continuity. Early marriage is not recommended, especially if it is based on sympathy. You may give your heart a little too readily on occasions.

Venus in Taurus

You are capable of very deep feelings and your emotions tend to last for a very long time. This makes you a trusting partner and lover, whose constancy is second to none. In life you are precise and careful and always try to do things the right way. Although this means an ordered life, which you are comfortable with, it can also lead you to be rather too fussy for your own good. Despite your pleasant nature, you are very fixed in your opinions and quite able to speak your mind. Others are attracted to you and historical astrologers always quoted this position of Venus as being very fortunate in terms of marriage. However, if you find yourself involved in a failed relationship, it could take you a long time to trust again.

Venus in Gemini

As with all associations related to Gemini, you tend to be quite versatile, anxious for change and intelligent in your dealings with the world at large. You may gain money from more than one source but you are equally good at spending it. There is an inference here that you are a good communicator, via either the written or the spoken word, and you love to be in the company of interesting people. Always on the look-out for culture, you may also be very fond of music, and love to indulge the curious and cultured side of your nature. In romance you tend to have more than one relationship and could find yourself associated with someone who has previously been a friend or even a distant relative.

Venus in Cancer

You often stay close to home because you are very fond of family and enjoy many of your most treasured moments when you are with those you love. Being naturally sympathetic, you will always do anything you can to support those around you, even people you hardly know at all. This charitable side of your nature is your most noticeable trait and is one of the reasons why others are naturally so fond of you. Being receptive and in some cases even psychic, you can see through to the soul of most of those with whom you come into contact. You may not commence too many romantic attachments but when you do give your heart, it tends to be unconditionally.

Venus in Leo

It must become quickly obvious to almost anyone you meet that you are kind, sympathetic and yet determined enough to stand up for anyone or anything that is truly important to you. Bright and sunny, you warm the world with your natural enthusiasm and would rarely do anything to hurt those around you, or at least not intentionally. In romance you are ardent and sincere, though some may find your style just a little overpowering. Gains come through your contacts with other people and this could be especially true with regard to romance, for love and money often come hand in hand for those who were born with Venus in Leo. People claim to understand you, though you are more complex than you seem.

Venus in Virgo

Your nature could well be fairly quiet no matter what your Sun sign might be, though this fact often manifests itself as an inner peace and would not prevent you from being basically sociable. Some delays and even the odd disappointment in love cannot be ruled out with this planetary position, though it's a fact that you will usually find the happiness you look for in the end. Catapulting yourself into romantic entanglements that you know to be rather ill-advised is not sensible, and it would be better to wait before you committed yourself exclusively to any one person. It is the essence of your nature to serve the world at large and through doing so it is possible that you will attract money at some stage in your life.

Venus in Libra

Venus is very comfortable in Libra and bestows upon those people who have this planetary position a particular sort of kindness that is easy to recognise. This is a very good position for all sorts of friendships and also for romantic attachments that usually bring much joy into your life. Few individuals with Venus in Libra would avoid marriage and since you are capable of great depths of love, it is likely that you will find a contented personal life. You like to mix with people of integrity and intelligence but don't take kindly to scruffy surroundings or work that means getting your hands too dirty. Careful speculation, good business dealings and money through marriage all seem fairly likely.

Venus in Scorpio

You are quite open and tend to spend money quite freely, even on those occasions when you don't have very much. Although your intentions are always good, there are times when you get yourself into the odd scrape and this can be particularly true when it comes to romance, which you may come to late or from a rather unexpected direction. Certainly you have the power to be happy and to make others contented on the way, but you find the odd stumbling block on your journey through life and it could seem that you have to work harder than those around you. As a result of this, you gain a much deeper understanding of the true value of personal happiness than many people ever do, and are likely to achieve true contentment.

Venus in Sagittarius

You are lighthearted, cheerful and always able to see the funny side of any situation. These facts enhance your popularity, which is especially high with members of the opposite sex. You should never have to look too far to find romantic interest in your life, though it is just possible that you might be too willing to commit yourself before you are certain that the person in question is right for you. Part of the problem here extends to other areas of life too. The fact is that you like variety in everything and so can tire of situations that fail to offer it. All the same, if you choose wisely and learn to understand your restless side, then great happiness can be yours.

Venus in Capricorn

The most notable trait that comes from Venus in this position is that it makes you trustworthy and able to take on all sorts of responsibilities in life. People are instinctively fond of you and love you all the more because you are always ready to help those who are in any form of need. Social and business popularity can be yours and there is a magnetic quality to your nature that is particularly attractive in a romantic sense. Anyone who wants a partner for a lover, a spouse and a good friend too would almost certainly look in your direction. Constancy is the hallmark of your nature and unfaithfulness would go right against the grain. You might sometimes be a little too trusting.

Venus in Aquarius

This location of Venus offers a fondness for travel and a desire to try out something new at every possible opportunity. You are extremely easy to get along with and tend to have many friends from varied backgrounds, classes and inclinations. You like to live a distinct sort of life and gain a great deal from moving about, both in a career sense and with regard to your home. It is not out of the question that you could form a romantic attachment to someone who comes from far away or be attracted to a person of a distinctly artistic and original nature. What you cannot stand is jealousy, for you have friends of both sexes and would want to keep things that way.

Venus in Pisces

The first thing people tend to notice about you is your wonderful, warm smile. Being very charitable by nature you will do anything to help others, even if you don't know them well. Much of your life may be spent sorting out situations for other people, but it is very important to feel that you are living for yourself too. In the main, you remain cheerful, and tend to be quite attractive to members of the opposite sex. Where romantic attachments are concerned, you could be drawn to people who are significantly older or younger than yourself or to someone with a unique career or point of view. It might be best for you to avoid marrying whilst you are still very young.

TAURUS:
2018 DIARY PAGES

2018

1 MONDAY
Moon Age Day 22   Moon Sign Gemini

Don't be surprised if some romantic overtures are coming your way at any time now. Most of these will come from expected directions. Avenues of communication now tend to open up after a few days when some Taureans may have felt quieter or more restricted in social situations, so make the most of this.

2 TUESDAY
Moon Age Day 23   Moon Sign Cancer

In the main you present a very humorous face to the world at large and there are likely to be many laughs along the way. Taurus occasionally takes itself rather more seriously than it should, though this definitely isn't the case now. Your thinking and the way you communicate are positive.

3 WEDNESDAY
Moon Age Day 24   Moon Sign Cancer

Getting to grips with family issues should be easy and you will also find sufficient time for romance to work one or two little wonders in your life. House and home suddenly appear very important, creating the right circumstances for a happy but deliberately family-focused sort of middle to the working week.

4 THURSDAY
Moon Age Day 25   Moon Sign Leo

Even casual friends can be particularly warm right now and there could be some surprising news arriving from the direction of a really close pal. Personal relationships should be working extremely well for you and some Taureans should be finding themselves at the start of exciting new romances.

5 FRIDAY *Moon Age Day 26   Moon Sign Leo*

Organising yourself might prove a little awkward today, though mainly in a humorous way. You have a tendency to be just a little absent-minded under present trends. You are most likely happily on the go for most of today, with travel once again positively highlighted and an ability to make gains in new places.

6 SATURDAY *Moon Age Day 27   Moon Sign Virgo*

Take a fresh look at old issues and be willing to address a point of view that is rather different from the one you might generally adopt yourself. You can put the force of your personality to good use right now, even though strictly professional or practical matters probably will not be on the agenda. This is Saturday after all.

7 SUNDAY *Moon Age Day 28   Moon Sign Virgo*

Make this Sunday your own by getting out of the house with relatives or friends and by seeking to push the margins of the possible. Your social life and group ventures generally are important at this stage and you should do everything within your power in order to enjoy yourself as much as you can.

8 MONDAY *Moon Age Day 29   Moon Sign Virgo*

There are good prospects for travel today, and it also appears that at work you now have more power at your fingertips and a better idea of how you should go about important tasks. People will call upon you for your special support. The more you get done today the better is your chance of enjoying some relaxation later in the week.

9 TUESDAY *Moon Age Day 0   Moon Sign Libra*

There are gains to be made on the financial front but you will need to be careful about investing any sum of money and consider all the options before you take any action. Friends should be very supportive and extremely loyal at this time. It won't be hard for you to trust people and you can rely on your intuition when it comes to sorting out the wheat from the chaff in any social situation.

10 WEDNESDAY   *Moon Age Day 1   Moon Sign Libra*

Your confidence remains high enough when you are dealing with practical matters, but you could be just slightly below par in your search for absolute personal happiness. Some positive benefits may arise from groups and partnerships. Although you do not always mix absolutely freely with the world at large, you will do so more readily now.

11 THURSDAY   *Moon Age Day 2   Moon Sign Scorpio*

Your enthusiasm is likely to flag now that the lunar low is around. This means that you won't be as optimistic as life and circumstances actually deserve. If you have to spend some money now in order to save later, then this is the course of action you should take. In social relationships avoid pushing matters to breaking point – there's really no need.

12 FRIDAY   *Moon Age Day 3   Moon Sign Scorpio*

It's time to slow down and take stock. If there are any jobs you really don't feel like doing today, leave them for later. Taking a well-earned break is no sin and you will work that much harder after the lunar low is gone. The attitudes of both family members and friends could be difficult to fathom today.

13 SATURDAY   *Moon Age Day 4   Moon Sign Sagittarius*

Things could get more exciting now. Your ideas and what might once have seemed your most outrageous schemes can find support from others today. This is partly because you are explaining yourself so well and you won't have any difficulty persuading people that you are quite a specialist in some ways. Keep abreast of current affairs.

14 SUNDAY   *Moon Age Day 5   Moon Sign Sagittarius*

Be gentle on yourself today. You won't get very far if you insist on trying to get ahead by sheer force. The force of your own personality provides all that is necessary to see you achieving more or less anything you want, but this is not a time for forcing issues. Taurus is very considerate of relatives and friends at this time.

15 MONDAY   *Moon Age Day 6   Moon Sign Capricorn*

It may now be possible to confront an issue that you have tried to avoid in the past, and this might be much easier than you had been expecting. Get jobs you don't like out of the way early. You should be especially pleased with your social life and with friendships, because both offer you diversion and interest today.

16 TUESDAY   *Moon Age Day 7   Moon Sign Capricorn*

Your luck with money certainly doesn't appear to have run out. Venus is now strong in your chart and ought to be reasonably supportive in financial terms. There are also possible gains on the work front. Some relationships need a new approach, which necessitates a change of attitude on your part.

17 WEDNESDAY   *Moon Age Day 8   Moon Sign Capricorn*

Consolidation seems to be the key to getting on well right now. Instead of firing off with new ideas, look carefully at the ones you have been addressing recently. It might take only a very small amount of effort to put the seal on weeks or months of work. On the way through life today new friends are a possibility.

18 THURSDAY   *Moon Age Day 9   Moon Sign Aquarius*

There is a powerful indication in your chart that money-making will rise to the forefront of your mind around this time. It may be for this reason that your associations with others are taking second place. If everything is firmly in place regarding the details of your life, your ability to make cash along the way goes without saying.

19 FRIDAY   *Moon Age Day 10   Moon Sign Aquarius*

The planetary emphasis now pushes you in the direction of work and property. That means you are taking less notice of friendship. This could be something of a mistake because there are definitely people around you now who want to get closer to you. With these contacts comes a whole new way of looking at certain matters.

20 SATURDAY
Moon Age Day 11   Moon Sign Pisces

Minor unexpected pressures are brought to bear on you now. These can do little to stem the general progress that surrounds you at present, though they could slow you down somewhat. Take care when dealing with younger family members, some of whom are far too sensitive for their own good.

21 SUNDAY
Moon Age Day 12   Moon Sign Pisces

This is a time during which love life and relationships should be putting a very definite smile on your face. If you don't have the time to do everything you wish in a practical sense, be willing to leave some of it for another day. Most of the people you meet today prove to be very reasonable.

22 MONDAY
Moon Age Day 13   Moon Sign Pisces

Don't believe everything you hear today because there are some unreliable types around. Mostly, these will be people who are charming and quite incapable of doing you any harm, but you need to be on your guard all the same. Trends also suggest a slight tendency towards mysterious little illnesses.

23 TUESDAY
Moon Age Day 14   Moon Sign Aries

Work and practical affairs keep you generally busy today and offer you the comfort of knowing that life is running in a smooth and steady way. There probably won't be too much in the way of excitement, though you are hardly likely to be put off by that fact at the moment.

24 WEDNESDAY
Moon Age Day 15   Moon Sign Aries

Although you are feeling quite assertive today, you do need to watch your step in some ways. Not everyone is working towards your ultimate good, no matter what they say to the contrary. Problems are not likely to arise with relatives or friends, though colleagues could be more of a problem.

25 THURSDAY   *Moon Age Day 16   Moon Sign Taurus*

Everything should be a laugh today and even situations you once found hard going are dealt with in a flash. Most of the people you meet seem to be naturally compromising in their attitudes but much of this has to do with the way you are feeling yourself. Your high spirits are evident, as is your sense of humour.

26 FRIDAY   *Moon Age Day 17   Moon Sign Taurus*

This is the time of the month during which you can afford to test your luck. The gains that can come along today could surpass your expectations and you certainly do need to make quick decisions if you want to make the very best of life. Confidence is written through you in a way that really shows.

27 SATURDAY   *Moon Age Day 18   Moon Sign Gemini*

Right now you have the knack of getting your point of view across in a very positive way and can really get on famously when in the company of people whose attitude stimulates you in any way. Frank, free and quite outspoken, you can definitely make today your own with only a little effort.

28 SUNDAY   *Moon Age Day 19   Moon Sign Gemini*

Now your acquisitive tendencies are strong, which isn't so strange for the zodiac sign of Taurus. You know what you want from life, and have a pretty good idea about how you intend to get it. Some would call you calculating, but since you bear the good of others in mind, this isn't really the case.

29 MONDAY   *Moon Age Day 20   Moon Sign Cancer*

Socially speaking, there are one or two individuals who could let you down today, which is why it would be sensible to check and double check all details. This is also true with regard to travel. Journeys might have to be postponed, or rearranged at the last minute.

30 TUESDAY   *Moon Age Day 21   Moon Sign Cancer*

There is likely to be a good deal of nostalgia in the air at this time. Looking back is fine, just as long as you don't always use aspects of the past as a yardstick for what is happening now. Times change and you alter with them. Keep an open mind about the behaviour and attitudes of younger family members.

31 WEDNESDAY   *Moon Age Day 22   Moon Sign Cancer*

Career issues should prove to be quite fulfilling. However, there are certain actions that you should be taking yourself in order to get ahead of the game. If people are not pulling their weight to the extent that you think is necessary, now is the time to remind them of the fact. Meanwhile, put in that extra bit of effort yourself.

November
2018

1 THURSDAY
Moon Age Day 23   Moon Sign Leo

There is help around if you want it, though you tend to be rather insular on occasions at the moment and might even think that to ask for assistance is beneath your dignity. A rather thorny problem could arise today and you need to be fairly circumspect in the way you choose to deal with it. You do have confidence – but you have to seek it within yourself.

2 FRIDAY
Moon Age Day 24   Moon Sign Leo

Friday brings a more energetic phase and the chance to get ahead, particularly at work. You are not lacking in know-how and might think up a new way to do something important. Be aware that people are watching you today, though in a very positive manner, so put your best foot forward.

3 SATURDAY
Moon Age Day 25   Moon Sign Virgo

Be willing to compromise today and others will relinquish a great deal of the control of situations to you. Taurus may not see itself as a natural leader, but those around you respect both your views and actions. This is likely to be a time that proves to be particularly good for social adventures and for general co-operation.

4 SUNDAY
Moon Age Day 26   Moon Sign Virgo

Getting on with others should not be difficult today, but you could find some people to be rather less decisive than you would wish. Don't try to please too many people because it simply won't work. It might be necessary to let those you love make their own mistakes since it is probably the only way they will learn valuable lessons.

5 MONDAY
Moon Age Day 27   Moon Sign Libra

Those in authority tend to be on your side at the start of this new working week and you should also find friends being especially helpful. Concentrate on a specific matter early in the day and generalities later. There could be one or two shortcuts to success for Taurus now, especially if you keep your eyes open.

6 TUESDAY
Moon Age Day 28   Moon Sign Libra

Despite the time of year, travel could be uppermost in your mind and if you are planning a long-term journey it might be sensible to speak to someone who knows the location well. Check and recheck all details before you embark. This is the best time of the week for conversation, even with people you have never met before.

7 WEDNESDAY
Moon Age Day 0   Moon Sign Scorpio

The attitudes and opinions of those you are dealing with on a daily basis might surprise or even shock you later in the day, but don't let on that this is the case. Keep your expectations of life realistic and the chances are that the lunar low won't have too much of a bearing on your life at this time.

8 THURSDAY
Moon Age Day 1   Moon Sign Scorpio

Progress may be steady at best because you have the lunar low to contend with today. This might not appear to be too much of a drag because you have been constantly on the go for a while now. All Taureans need rest and recuperation at some stage because that is what gets you thinking and planning.

9 FRIDAY
Moon Age Day 2   Moon Sign Sagittarius

Avoid family disputes and it might be sensible to spend as much time as you can with people to whom you are not related at all. Although you could suffer from a slight lack of inspiration early in the day, it won't be long before you are feeling much more positive and really getting stuck into things.

10 SATURDAY   *Moon Age Day 3   Moon Sign Sagittarius*

Not everyone appears to have your best interests at heart but it is possible that in a few cases you are misinterpreting the situation. A better day for finances is possible, perhaps with some unexpected gains. Group events give today an air of excitement and it is very easy for you to join in and have fun.

11 SUNDAY   *Moon Age Day 4   Moon Sign Sagittarius*

Not everyone shares your opinions at the moment, but you are not likely to contradict anyone today. It looks as though you are keeping yourself very much to yourself. You won't be thinking big because present trends favour the smaller world-view that comes over Taurus on occasions. Money matters should be variable but generally stable.

12 MONDAY   *Moon Age Day 5   Moon Sign Capricorn*

Visits to family members or even friends you don't see very often might prove to be especially rewarding and you seem to be in a particularly social frame of mind all of a sudden. The conversations you have with others around this time tend to be pleasant and sympathetic in both directions.

13 TUESDAY   *Moon Age Day 6   Moon Sign Capricorn*

It is in a professional sense that the competitive qualities of your nature are on display. You need this hard edge on occasions, but it's impossible domestically right now. Enjoy the fact that you can take a different and more stimulating approach in discussions at work, while those at home are somehow sugar-coated at the moment.

14 WEDNESDAY   *Moon Age Day 7   Moon Sign Aquarius*

In love and relationships you need to use your intuition today. Perhaps your partner is not behaving as you have come to expect or else the object of your devotion still isn't noticing you? There's more than one way to skin a cat and when it comes to being slightly devious, you have what it takes at the moment. Use your powers of communication as they are looking good.

15 THURSDAY   *Moon Age Day 8   Moon Sign Aquarius*

The really positive part of today is likely to come along once your commitments in the practical world are out of the way. Meanwhile a change in planetary emphasis today means inevitable alterations to your working schedules. Not all of these look potentially good but will probably work out better than you expect.

16 FRIDAY   *Moon Age Day 9   Moon Sign Aquarius*

Taking a very serious attitude to almost anything right now could turn out to be something of a mistake. The more off-the-wall you appear to be at present, the greater is the attention you get. Exercise a little caution because certain important changes you have been gradually making to your life might now come temporarily unstuck.

17 SATURDAY   ☿   *Moon Age Day 10   Moon Sign Pisces*

Everyday life is apt to be pleasant and rewarding, with personal relationships offering the best possibilities of all this Saturday. You can make life go with a swing for family members, and most of all for your partner. It should also be possible to speculate rather more than you have been doing earlier in the week, with caution of course.

18 SUNDAY   ☿   *Moon Age Day 11   Moon Sign Pisces*

Challenges, or even confrontations, in your closest personal relationships may threaten to shake your equilibrium somewhat. This is only really an issue if you allow yourself to be drawn in. Try to remain patient, even in the face of criticism, and all should be well. On a positive note, your finances could be strengthening at this time.

19 MONDAY   ☿   *Moon Age Day 12   Moon Sign Aries*

A fairly nostalgic day is certain now, with time also for reflection on happenings early in the month. Once again it is particularly important not to dwell on things that have been and gone. If you are using your view of past events in order to explain your present activities, there is a strong chance that you are not committing yourself fully.

20 TUESDAY ☿ *Moon Age Day 13   Moon Sign Aries*

Although you are intellectually quicker than ever, there are still one or two people around who seem to want to fool you in some way. This is going to be difficult for them to achieve because you are clearly on the ball and attentive today. Make the most of this time to ring the changes socially and personally.

21 WEDNESDAY ☿ *Moon Age Day 14   Moon Sign Taurus*

This is a good time to push your luck and certainly not a period during which you should hide your abilities or your intentions. Allow your light to shine brightly and have confidence in your ability to get things done. Financial trends are especially good, as are the romantic prospects of this positive day.

22 THURSDAY ☿ *Moon Age Day 15   Moon Sign Taurus*

Your confidence is greatly increased and there is no doubt about your desire to get ahead. This may not be immediately obvious at work but you are very good at mixing business with pleasure right now. Ideal situations might just happen by themselves – but a little push from you won't do any harm either.

23 FRIDAY ☿ *Moon Age Day 16   Moon Sign Taurus*

A new boost to your romantic life comes along now. Concentrate more on the relationship that you have with your partner and spend time in their company. If this is difficult on account of work commitments, you can at least find some moments later in the day to let those you love know how much you care.

24 SATURDAY ☿ *Moon Age Day 17   Moon Sign Gemini*

Some setbacks could be unavoidable today. It would be best not to bite off more than you can chew and to allow your friends and colleagues to do some jobs on your behalf. There is nothing at all wrong with looking ahead and doing a little careful planning, whilst at the same time getting some rest.

25 SUNDAY ☿ *Moon Age Day 18 Moon Sign Gemini*

Friendship and group encounters generally appear to have a great deal going for them right now. What they provide is a platform for your ego, perhaps at a time when you are not quite as confident in yourself as has been the case of late. Make time to socialise, particularly by the evening.

26 MONDAY ☿ *Moon Age Day 19 Moon Sign Cancer*

Today you find a positive emphasis being placed on material considerations. This is the sort of month November is turning out to be for you and you take great delight in new possessions. Don't forget before you spend money that Christmas is not that far away.

27 TUESDAY ☿ *Moon Age Day 20 Moon Sign Cancer*

After a somewhat busy period, you might be feeling slightly overtaxed and will probably be pleased enough to have a restful day or two. Whether things turn out that way really depends on how willing you are to allow others to take some of the strain. Actually, it might be churlish to prevent them.

28 WEDNESDAY ☿ *Moon Age Day 21 Moon Sign Leo*

At work, someone may be putting you in the picture regarding an issue that has been at the forefront of your mind of late. Getting to know what is going on in your vicinity seems especially important now, which is why you are listening so carefully to everything that is being said.

29 THURSDAY ☿ *Moon Age Day 22 Moon Sign Leo*

You have little real patience with certain emotional matters today and you may consider that someone you know well is acting in a fairly irrational manner. There are some unusual people about, whose ideas and actions could fascinate you somewhat, but don't be drawn into anything weird.

30 FRIDAY   ☿   *Moon Age Day 23   Moon Sign Virgo*

The domestic atmosphere is likely to become livelier, with much communication taking place and a possible visit from relatives or friends. For today you can expect a number of surprises and unbidden events, all of which contribute to a general increase in interest and participation on your part.

♉ December
2018

1 SATURDAY ☿ *Moon Age Day 24 Moon Sign Virgo*

Spend time with family members and do what you can to support a friend who could well be going through a rough phase right now. You are well aware of the elements of your life that deserve your attention, even though one or two people might think that they know different.

2 SUNDAY ☿ *Moon Age Day 25 Moon Sign Libra*

Well ahead of the holiday season could be as good a time as any to analyse what you have achieved during the last year and to make new plans for beyond the end of December. Certainly, you are likely to have the time to do so, on what could prove to be a somewhat quieter day. Trends do suggest, though, that you haven't seen for a long time could come back into your life.

3 MONDAY ☿ *Moon Age Day 26 Moon Sign Libra*

For many Taureans the time is right for a short break from obligations. Maybe you have some time off work, or at least are relinquishing a few of the responsibilities that you would normally take on. For whatever reason, you have the chance for a steadier day, and will probably grab it with both hands.

4 TUESDAY ☿ *Moon Age Day 27 Moon Sign Scorpio*

Get ready for a couple of days during which it will be difficult to get everything you want from life. The lunar low is holding you back, but not all that much. As long as you stick to planning, and leave a few of the more concrete jobs until the back end of the week, you will hardly be held up at all this month.

5 WEDNESDAY ☿ *Moon Age Day 28 Moon Sign Scorpio*

You are trying very hard to swim against a tide that really will not turn in your favour. Maybe it should have occurred to you by now that this is a complete waste of time and effort. Let someone else take the strain for the moment, whilst you sit back and enjoy yourself. Taurus can enjoy a really clear conscience now.

6 THURSDAY ☿ *Moon Age Day 29 Moon Sign Scorpio*

You won't be very pleased with yourself if situations become confused or if you are not keeping up with the expectations others have of you. In a more general sense, you ought to be feeling quite positive about life. The main thing today is keeping on top of organisational issues.

7 FRIDAY *Moon Age Day 0 Moon Sign Sagittarius*

Certain planetary trends show this to be a time during which Taurus becomes fascinated by the way things work. Some experimentation is called for, if only to satisfy your curiosity. The spirit of teamwork is stronger in you today and your ability to get on well with the world at large is more noticeable.

8 SATURDAY *Moon Age Day 1 Moon Sign Sagittarius*

It might be necessary to fend off one or two social invitations today, if only because you can't do everything. Gathering together all the relevant information you need should be child's play now. You are particularly well organised at the moment, which is probably why others turn to you when they need sorting out.

9 SUNDAY *Moon Age Day 2 Moon Sign Capricorn*

It could just be that you feel you cannot break through the carefully created shell of a colleague or friend. However, there are great rewards to be had from even the most mundane aspects of life, even if you have to look at matters carefully and use a good deal of intuition to get the best from any situation.

10 MONDAY *Moon Age Day 3 Moon Sign Capricorn*

A sense of variety and freedom is both important and appealing to Taureans at this time. Don't be a stick-in-the-mud. Although this might not be exactly the season for outdoor activities, you could find the call of the wild appealing. Later in the day, you might choose to spend at least some time alone.

11 TUESDAY *Moon Age Day 4 Moon Sign Aquarius*

The present emphasis falls on finances, probably not surprising at this expensive time of the year. You are quite canny at the moment and know full well how to get value for money. Even at this stage, there could be one or two things available for Christmas that you get at rock bottom prices.

12 WEDNESDAY *Moon Age Day 5 Moon Sign Aquarius*

Be willing to take a few chances and to push the bounds of credibility when it comes to your own ideas. Romance looms large in your thinking and compliments are not hard to come by. Although you might feel that your influence over everyday matters is rather limited, you would probably be wrong.

13 THURSDAY *Moon Age Day 6 Moon Sign Aquarius*

For many Taureans, the greatest joy of today comes from your love life, which is likely to be as enjoyable as you would wish. Something you have done for someone else in the past is now paid back with dividends. Expecting the best of others is worthwhile at present since they are unlikely to let you down.

14 FRIDAY *Moon Age Day 7 Moon Sign Pisces*

Along comes a happy period during which you should find yourself to be the centre of attention. Although such a situation would sometimes cause embarrassment to the Taurus nature, that isn't at all the case now. Avoid confusion in your associations with others by simply speaking your mind with candour.

15 SATURDAY
Moon Age Day 8   Moon Sign Pisces

Try to avoid needless arguments with your friends. Even if people seem to be in the most intractable frame of mind you don't have to join in. Make this a Saturday to remember by doing something different. If this turns out to be a problem, look to your most exciting and original friend for ideas.

16 SUNDAY
Moon Age Day 9   Moon Sign Pisces

There are new and interesting people around and they seem to come along at just the right time as far as you are concerned. There may be tasks to do today that you like the look of at all. All the same, you should avoid putting them off because you might be making a rod for your own back later.

17 MONDAY
Moon Age Day 10   Moon Sign Aries

What an excellent day this would be for getting something new up and running. Positive trends seem to be assisting in most of your efforts and there could also be financial gains, both expected and surprising. You can call on a creative mood and lightness of touch just when you need it the most.

18 TUESDAY
Moon Age Day 11   Moon Sign Aries

You score many points in social situations, particularly if you are away from home and enjoying the hospitality of others. Try not to be critical about the way those around you arrange their functions and simply pitch in. Too much fussing won't get you anywhere today so try to stay very relaxed.

19 WEDNESDAY
Moon Age Day 12   Moon Sign Taurus

Almost never will you notice the onset of the lunar high more than appears to be the case today. Things have been quite up and down across the last week or so, but it's plain today that you are ready for action and quite keen to get ahead. Don't worry about how you do things, simply get stuck in.

20 THURSDAY
Moon Age Day 13   Moon Sign Taurus

This is when you reach your mental and physical peak, just in time for the last run-up to Christmas. It doesn't matter what you take on today, you have the energy and determination to see it through properly. Gains can be made as a result of meetings and discussions that could have taken place some time ago.

21 FRIDAY
Moon Age Day 14   Moon Sign Gemini

You may be in two minds about certain issues today, especially those connected with work. If this turns out to be the case you really need to use your intuition, which is working well at this time. Avoid getting into any sort of difficulty by varying your routines and also by thinking about things in different ways.

22 SATURDAY
Moon Age Day 15   Moon Sign Gemini

Financially speaking, there could be some minor improvements on the horizon now, and not a moment too soon with Christmas so close. Nevertheless, you need to spend wisely and to look out for those bargains that lie around every corner. All in all, this could be one of the best days of December for shopping.

23 SUNDAY
Moon Age Day 16   Moon Sign Cancer

You may be feeling quite restless today, though it would be difficult for you to know exactly why this state of affairs has come about. You could blame any number of possibilities but that is no excuse for not treating others properly. Get rid of your own strange thoughts by concentrating on the lives of those around you.

24 MONDAY
Moon Age Day 17   Moon Sign Cancer

You should definitely be enjoying a high profile on this Christmas Eve. Despite the fact that you register how much still has to be done, you must find ways in which you can enjoy yourself. If you keep slogging away for the whole of the day you will be left with the impression that everyone is having fun at your expense.

25 TUESDAY
Moon Age Day 18   Moon Sign Leo

In all probability you will enjoy an extremely interesting and varied sort of Christmas Day. It could be that not everyone in your family and friendship circle is having quite as good a time as you are and this might lead to extra effort on your part. The most enjoyable associations today come via close, personal attachments.

26 WEDNESDAY
Moon Age Day 19   Moon Sign Leo

Almost everyone wants your attention at the same time today. The personal need to be busy and active might run contrary to all the festive celebrations now. What you need to do is compartmentalise your time, making sure that you have at least some moments left to spend with your partner and with family members.

27 THURSDAY
Moon Age Day 20   Moon Sign Virgo

Affairs of the heart are well highlighted in your chart today, as is travel, perhaps to see people you haven't shared an hour or two with for quite a long time. Although you might be bullied into doing things that go against the grain, you could be quite surprised with how they turn out in the end. It is worth putting yourself out.

28 FRIDAY
Moon Age Day 21   Moon Sign Virgo

Now it appears you are in such a hurry to get things done, you are forgetting some of the most important details. If you want to avoid having to stop, and then begin all over again, concentrate fully on the task at hand. Friends are there to lend a helping hand if you offer them the chance to do so.

29 SATURDAY
Moon Age Day 22   Moon Sign Libra

This is far from being a normal sort of Saturday as far as you are concerned, even if you have to work. When you are not busy, there are gains to be made through love and new friendship. Your social instincts are very definitely engaged today and you can be the best company imaginable. You not only join in but should be happy to organise things too.

30 SUNDAY
Moon Age Day 23   Moon Sign Libra

With the positive emphasis this Sunday on your inner self, and maybe also on your personal life, the sort of entertaining aspects of recent days don't appeal to the same extent. The result may seem to be a seesaw quality to your nature. It can't be helped, that's the way the planets are for you right now.

31 MONDAY
Moon Age Day 24   Moon Sign Libra

The chances are that your enthusiasm is at a peak and this is certainly no bad way to end a year. All you are really interested in today is having fun, together with making it possible for those around you to have a good time too. New Year resolutions may be put on hold, because the enjoyment is hardly likely to stop at midnight.

TAURUS:
2019 DIARY PAGES

TAURUS:
YOUR YEAR IN BRIEF

There are jobs to be done at the start of this year that you probably will not like the look of, but the astrological advice for January and February is to get stuck in as soon as possible. Once the dross is out of the way, you can get on with what you really want to do. Someone you don't see often may return to your life and there may also be more opportunities for travel than you might normally expect so early in the year. If you are involved in sport, push yourself and really go for gold.

Things might slow down a little during March and April, but you should keep putting in that extra effort that makes all the difference to your zodiac sign. If some people around you are in a low-key mood, or family issues are on your mind don't let this drag you down.

May and June bring the start of the summer and a chance for Taurus to really start moving. It is at this time of year that you generally do best and at the moment you should be filled with boundless energy. You may have to be careful not to upset colleagues or friends during June and it would be sensible for you to check and double check details before embarking on long-distance travel.

With the arrival of the high summer there isn't much doubt that you will want to be on the move. This is just as likely in a domestic sense as it will be in terms of holiday travel. July and August both bring ever-changing vistas and a greater sense of self-belief that is everything to your zodiac sign. Now is also the best time of the year to take on a new challenge – probably professional, but maybe personal.

September and October are filled with opportunities but of a low-key sort. Working at a slower pace, you won't be afraid to close certain chapters in your life. This looks likely to be more about getting things settled in your mind than starting new ventures. Some plans may have to be re-scheduled or postponed, but the things that come along by chance are the best events.

The final two months of the year, November and December, turn out to be a mixed bag for Taureans. Throughout November you may be feeling hemmed in because you can't do everything you wish. December should be quite different because you are looking and acting at your very best. Stay away from pointless routines and enjoy the holiday period for what it is worth. Don't worry about planning for 2019, because the start of next year will bring a higher degree of flexibility into your life as a whole.

January

(8)

2019

1 TUESDAY
Moon Age Day 25   Moon Sign Scorpio

You should not expect any active progress on this New Year's Day, but that doesn't mean that you are standing still. It's just as important to lay the foundations for new enterprises and you are generally quite happy to spend a Bank Holiday doing some planning. You find that you take a decision today that has tremendous implications further down the line.

2 WEDNESDAY
Moon Age Day 26   Moon Sign Scorpio

This is the second day of the monthly lunar low, the time when the Moon enters your opposite zodiac sign, and you don't really have what it takes to get ahead for today at least. Instead, rely on the help and support of some important people in your life and bask in the joy that romance can bring. The trends in a day or two will be better.

3 THURSDAY
Moon Age Day 27   Moon Sign Sagittarius

As the Moon moves on, you should be in a much better position to call the shots, not least because those closest to you, especially at work, are more than happy to follow your lead. Avoid anxiety over issues you cannot influence and be willing to give a friend the benefit of the doubt.

4 FRIDAY
Moon Age Day 28   Moon Sign Sagittarius

Present personal ambitions should be on their way to fruition. You might have to work that bit harder to get others to see the way you are feeling and that will mean speaking out. It isn't always easy for you to find the right words, but this should not be much of an issue.

5 SATURDAY   *Moon Age Day 0   Moon Sign Capricorn*

Trends suggest that you could be concerned about specific issues at the moment, perhaps even to the exclusion of all else. This approach really isn't good for you and it would be far better to take a broader view of life. If you manage this, things should work out for the better. As it's a weekend you may have the opportunity to change things up.

6 SUNDAY   *Moon Age Day 1   Moon Sign Capricorn*

Your mind is now likely to be anywhere except focused on the task in hand. This is not necessarily a bad thing. It merely means that you are able to think across a broad range of possibilities. You may even find new and revolutionary ways of doing jobs that were awkward or perhaps tedious before.

7 MONDAY   *Moon Age Day 2   Moon Sign Capricorn*

This is likely to be a better day and you can get your own way, mostly without seeming to try very hard. It is likely that you have shown great kindness to others recently and you may now find that you are rewarded for this in some way. Show family members how much you care about them and enjoy some romantic moments.

8 TUESDAY   *Moon Age Day 3   Moon Sign Aquarius*

Despite the persistent winter weather, it seems likely that you will want to get out of doors if you get the chance today. You have a hankering to be in the fresh air and as long as you are well wrapped up the change and the exercise will do you good and could also bring some excitement to an otherwise steady day.

9 WEDNESDAY   *Moon Age Day 4   Moon Sign Aquarius*

The wheels of progress turn on, sometimes even despite the fact that you don't seem to be contributing too much. Financially it appears that you are now dealing with situations one at a time. Taurus is coming into its own, especially when particularly important decisions need to be made.

10 THURSDAY
Moon Age Day 5   Moon Sign Pisces

Taureans are not people who shy away from a challenge, and it is possible that you could face one at the moment. It shouldn't be difficult to get what you want from life right now and there should be plenty of support around if you are in the market for it. Friends may occasionally have their own agenda, but you can cope with that.

11 FRIDAY
Moon Age Day 6   Moon Sign Pisces

Today marks a time when you can get much enjoyment simply from being amongst familiar faces. Less outgoing than you have been for the past few days, spending some time on your own might appeal to you. A certain degree of bravado is still present for those situations when it is necessary and you tend to smile a lot.

12 SATURDAY
Moon Age Day 7   Moon Sign Pisces

Any sort of travel, together with all intellectual pursuits is well highlighted by present trends. Staying in the same place for too long could prove to be quite tedious and so you may gain greatly by keeping your options open and moving around freely. A more free and easy sort of Taurus is beginning to show.

13 SUNDAY
Moon Age Day 8   Moon Sign Aries

Present planetary positions bring a potentially busy time and a period when you can gain from the viewpoints of friends and colleagues alike. Right now you are able to elicit the best from those around you, many of whom will want to assist you for no reason other than that they like you so much.

14 MONDAY
Moon Age Day 9   Moon Sign Aries

Although getting ahead at work might seem to present a few problems, you won't be stuck for some good ideas. Mentally and physically you should now be on a peak and ready to reap some rewards as a result of your past efforts. Taurus is always much stronger and more robust than it considers itself to be.

15 TUESDAY   *Moon Age Day 10   Moon Sign Taurus*

Today brings the lunar high and a time during which you are bright, happy and likely to see the best in everything and everyone. Your energy levels will be high and you may sense that good luck is on your side. Plan now for some quite far-reaching practical changes you want to make as early as tomorrow.

16 WEDNESDAY   *Moon Age Day 11   Moon Sign Taurus*

This should be a good day and one during which you have everything you need to make the best possible impression, not least of all on people who really count. There are gains to be made financially and also with regard to romance. Don't be too quick to make a judgement of your own past efforts. They are better than you think.

17 THURSDAY   *Moon Age Day 12   Moon Sign Taurus*

You are going to have to tell a few white lies if you really want to get your own way today. This sort of behaviour may not come easily to you, though there are planetary trends around that can help. Anything really old or distinctly curious is apt to appeal to you during the remainder of this week.

18 FRIDAY   *Moon Age Day 13   Moon Sign Gemini*

Conserve some of your energy because the social trends are getting better and better. If you wear yourself out during the day, you won't have either the drive or the initiative to make the most of what the evening has to offer. Whatever the weather, it's important to get plenty of fresh air now.

19 SATURDAY   *Moon Age Day 14   Moon Sign Gemini*

Keep up the pressure in professional matters if you are a weekend worker. If this isn't the case, find ways to enjoy yourself. Most Taureans like to keep busy and with your creative potential good at the moment, it isn't out of the question that you will be decorating your home or helping with projects at a friend's house.

20 SUNDAY
Moon Age Day 15   Moon Sign Cancer

Little unexpected gains may be right there for the taking today. While it's hardly likely you will become a millionaire overnight, if you keep your wits about you there is a possibility you could take the first step. You are never anyone's fool but at the moment your perceptions are razor sharp. Use your strong intuition when assessing others.

21 MONDAY
Moon Age Day 16   Moon Sign Cancer

You could be feeling very motivated today, especially during the afternoon and evening. If you are experiencing a surge of wanderlust, now is the time to exploit that by taking a journey. Don't be too quick to judge younger family members, no matter how they seem to be behaving.

22 TUESDAY
Moon Age Day 17   Moon Sign Leo

Stay away from get-rich-quick schemes today. Your intuition tells you that there is a good chance you will get your fingers burned and, while this is always sound advice, there isn't much doubt that this could be the case under present trends. A new hobby could be more to your liking at the moment, especially if it is one that has a physical dimension.

23 WEDNESDAY
Moon Age Day 18   Moon Sign Leo

A situation that requires you to rely heavily on others won't sit very well with you at all today. You are always an independent type and this trait is particularly highlighted under current trends. In social settings you shine much more than usual, but it is clear you prefer to be at the head of all matters now.

24 THURSDAY
Moon Age Day 19   Moon Sign Virgo

Your personality profile at the moment shows that you are slightly more difficult to fathom than you might have been earlier in the month. Be as open as you can and make it plain to people that you are not worrying about anything. When Taurus withdraws, it can be a problematic zodiac sign to understand.

25 FRIDAY
Moon Age Day 20   Moon Sign Virgo

Stick to paths you understand for the moment but prepare yourself for a major push before long. This might seem an uneventful sort of day but it is the things that are happening below the surface you should be watching carefully. It also seems likely that close personal ties should be working well for you now.

26 SATURDAY
Moon Age Day 21   Moon Sign Libra

Along comes Saturday and you probably are not prepared for the potential success that is just around the corner for you. If you do make progress now, it is likely to be as a result of things you did in the past, perhaps a long time ago. Don't hold back when people really want to know what you think about specific matters.

27 SUNDAY
Moon Age Day 22   Moon Sign Libra

This might be a day for making lists. Specific planetary trends incline you to be more absent-minded than would normally be the case. Just as long as you review matters early in the day to avoid forgetting anything important, you should be able to proceed normally. Family gatherings are distinctly possible at present.

28 MONDAY
Moon Age Day 23   Moon Sign Scorpio

There probably won't be a great deal of spare time today. Life is busy and you feel a good deal of pressure being placed upon your shoulders. You can deal with this so much better if you are prepare for all eventualities in a certain situation. What you really need to avoid is being surprised by issues you don't understand.

29 TUESDAY
Moon Age Day 24   Moon Sign Scorpio

Even when others virtually prove that you are wrong, you are unlikely to change either your stance or your actions unless they are really able to demonstrate their case to you. You have energy to spare so it would be sensible to do anything you can today instead of putting off tasks until a later date.

30 WEDNESDAY *Moon Age Day 25   Moon Sign Sagittarius*

Keep up the effort on all fronts. Even things you have had great difficulty doing in the past should come that much easier today. If you have to enlist the help and support of friends or colleagues, simply turn on the charm. It's doubtful that anyone could turn down a reasonable request from your direction at present.

31 THURSDAY *Moon Age Day 26   Moon Sign Sagittarius*

You now tend to be pushier and always eager to get ahead. Not everyone will behave in quite the way you either expect or plan, which can be the fly in the ointment for some of your schemes. You do, however, have great resilience and won't easily be dissuaded from taking actions you feel to be right.

⑧ February
2019

1 FRIDAY
Moon Age Day 27   Moon Sign Sagittarius

The last day of the working week for many of you could be the most important. This is a pivotal time and a period during which you are putting the finishing touches to some very important plans. Don't leave your work alone until you are sure you have everything sorted to your satisfaction.

2 SATURDAY
Moon Age Day 28   Moon Sign Capricorn

You definitely do want to be the best all the time at the moment and consequently may be quite disappointed if you fall short of your own expectations. There are plenty of people around who think you are quite marvellous and that helps but it won't be enough if you suspect you could be doing even better than you are.

3 SUNDAY
Moon Age Day 29   Moon Sign Capricorn

This could be quite a productive day in the financial sphere and a time when you should be feeling safe and secure. You have your own efforts to thank for this state of affairs – together with a little help from your family and friends. It might be good to take the time out today to acknowledge their support.

4 MONDAY
Moon Age Day 0   Moon Sign Aquarius

You can now take constructive action to expand your financial successes and may use specific situations to feather your own nest. However, you won't be forgetting about the more personal side of life and it looks as though romance could be well to the forefront of your mind at present.

5 TUESDAY
Moon Age Day 1   Moon Sign Aquarius

A time of discrimination and organisation is at hand. You see things very clearly today and there are no shades of grey in your life at all. Later in the day you may be overtaken by a more nostalgic frame of mind and could so easily be reliving a few minor regrets left over from the dim and distant past. Try not to let these concerns get on top of you, though.

6 WEDNESDAY
Moon Age Day 2   Moon Sign Aquarius

Opportunities may present themselves today for you to communicate your personal ideas with great authority. This is important because even if you don't know exactly what you are talking about, others will never guess that this is the case. Keep up your present efforts to lend assistance to good friends.

7 THURSDAY
Moon Age Day 3   Moon Sign Pisces

You could find yourself drawn to expensive and glamorous articles today. This happens to everyone now and again and is quite usual for Taurus. A love of luxury is sometimes present in you but is often a response to insecurity. Maybe you need to look at what is happening in and around your personal life?

8 FRIDAY
Moon Age Day 4   Moon Sign Pisces

You are able to express yourself with a great deal of conviction today and few people will be left in any doubt whatsoever about the way you are feeling. The attitude of friends can be somewhat puzzling and might lead you to asking a few leading questions in your search to help your pals out of a pickle.

9 SATURDAY
Moon Age Day 5   Moon Sign Aries

You are thoughtful and considerate of the feelings of others, which in turn inclines them to be extra pleasant to you. This is just as likely when you are dealing with strangers as it would be with those you know well. Don't be intimidated if you feel just slightly out of you depth right now.

10 SUNDAY · Moon Age Day 6 · Moon Sign Aries

There could be something of a conflict between personal desires and your ability to focus your mind on more abstract issues. This won't be too difficult to solve because your ability to concentrate is one of your real strengths. The demands and expectations of those around you have to be taken into account around now.

11 MONDAY · Moon Age Day 7 · Moon Sign Aries

Positive influences should now prevail in personal and family matters. You will enjoy the company of certain people enormously and may find yourself once again striking up a relationship that was important to you in the remote past. Your confidence in your ability to get what you want from life remains generally high.

12 TUESDAY · Moon Age Day 8 · Moon Sign Taurus

This would be a great time to push for what you really want from life. There are people around who seem more or less determined to help you out and your own popularity should assure you of a good day socially. You can afford to push your luck somewhat and remain very intuitive at present.

13 WEDNESDAY · Moon Age Day 9 · Moon Sign Taurus

This is your time and you don't have to defer to others, simply because they 'appear' to know more about situations than you do. Your influence is strong and getting the better of people who have used you in the past is something you should relish. However, you will not be at all spiteful towards them because that isn't your way.

14 THURSDAY · Moon Age Day 10 · Moon Sign Gemini

Differences of opinion can result in confrontation, something you would almost certainly rather avoid at the moment, especially if it's with a partner on Valentine's Day! There are occasions when this simply isn't possible so prepare yourself. If a disagreement is inevitable, make sure you settle matters quickly.

15 FRIDAY
Moon Age Day 11   Moon Sign Gemini

Certain people might accuse you of being rather selfish today but this is only likely to be the case with regard to individuals who are not doing quite as well for themselves as you are. Don't ignore the situation, but there is only so much you can do to make those around you feel entirely comfortable.

16 SATURDAY
Moon Age Day 12   Moon Sign Cancer

Something inside you is screaming that you should be putting your point of view forward more strongly, and that is certainly the case at work. If you are looking for a job at the moment, today could be a good time to make further enquiries. There might not be much excitement about, but there is potential gain.

17 SUNDAY
Moon Age Day 13   Moon Sign Cancer

Your wit is still showing strongly. You have a great ability to make almost anyone laugh today and if there is something you have to complain about, you do so with humour. Rules and regulations are inclined to get on your nerves right now, that is if you don't simply decide to ignore them altogether.

18 MONDAY
Moon Age Day 14   Moon Sign Leo

You have an amazing ability to go straight to the heart of just about any matter now. It would be great if you could decide to take today off work because you are also feeling somewhat hemmed in by responsibility and general circumstances. What you seem to need most of all now is a temporary change of scene.

19 TUESDAY
Moon Age Day 15   Moon Sign Leo

Standing up for your rights and for those of the people you care for seems to be very important at present, but so is making sure you have something to complain about before you get cracking. Checking details is crucial in every sphere of your life today and particularly so in travel arrangements.

20 WEDNESDAY   *Moon Age Day 16   Moon Sign Virgo*

Anything to do with modern technology not only attracts you at the moment but also shows how your mind tends to work. You can be very logical and arrive at some startling conclusions today as a result. Try to get away from too many family-based domestic routines.

21 THURSDAY   *Moon Age Day 17   Moon Sign Virgo*

If there is something you don't like today, ignore it. This isn't usually the sort of advice that would be offered to Taurus, but it is highly likely that you are now getting yourself into a state about nothing. Clear your head by taking a long walk and give some thought to long-term changes in your career.

22 FRIDAY   *Moon Age Day 18   Moon Sign Libra*

For many Taureans, the end of this working week means putting in that extra bit of effort that is going to prove so worthwhile next week. By the evening, you will be ready to party and that might mean getting together with friends. Your sparkling personality is on display and marks you out for extra attention.

23 SATURDAY   *Moon Age Day 19   Moon Sign Libra*

You are well ahead of the competition in some respects, even though it may look as if others are making more progress than you are. What is required is a little patience and confidence in your own past decisions. There are times during this part of the weekend when it is vital for you to keep your nerve.

24 SUNDAY   *Moon Age Day 20   Moon Sign Scorpio*

There could be some blocks on progress today, whether or not you work at the weekend. The lunar low has the power this time round to sap your resolve somewhat, though appreciating what is causing your state of mind is half way to defeating it. Take some time out to spend with your lover and your family.

25 MONDAY   *Moon Age Day 21   Moon Sign Scorpio*

Some things just refuse to go as you have planned today and there isn't any getting away from the fact. If necessary, you can start again tomorrow and redo whatever is necessary. This might not turn out to be a bad thing at all because you will be infinitely more successful second time around.

26 TUESDAY   *Moon Age Day 22   Moon Sign Sagittarius*

You should be getting on fine in a general sense, despite the fact that you don't have quite the level of self-belief that you deserve. Constant attention to detail could get on your nerves right now, which is why a change of task at work or at home would be as good as a rest. If you have time to conduct a general review of life, this could work out well for you.

27 WEDNESDAY *Moon Age Day 23   Moon Sign Sagittarius*

Now less inclined to look back to past situations, you are gradually growing more confident in your own vision of the future. That cannot be said to be the case for everyone around you, though your persuasive skills could make all the difference to people with a negative mindset. Believe and you can have almost anything now.

28 THURSDAY   *Moon Age Day 24   Moon Sign Sagittarius*

You are definitely working at your best in an intellectual sense. You would be especially good at any sort of competitions now and should positively excel at IQ tests. Maybe you should take a look at yourself in order to really understand on how many different levels your versatile mind can function.

March

2019

1 FRIDAY
Moon Age Day 25   Moon Sign Capricorn

You may be happy to settle for average progress today. Trends indicate that you might fear the presence of some people who have a vested interest in preventing you from getting ahead. In reality this is almost certainly not the case, but if it is possible for you to get hold of the wrong end of the stick you are likely to do so under present trends.

2 SATURDAY
Moon Age Day 26   Moon Sign Capricorn

Your best romantic intentions may turn out to be less successful than you hoped, probably because of the attitude of your target. Some rethinking may be necessary as a result and you could need to try a different approach. One thing is for certain: if you have made up your mind about something, you won't let anything put you off.

3 SUNDAY
Moon Age Day 27   Moon Sign Aquarius

If new possibilities present themselves you should be looking beyond simple curiosity and towards the most practical way to apply yourself to them. Give yourself a pat on the back for recent successes, but avoid complacency. This ought to be a comfortable time materially.

4 MONDAY
Moon Age Day 28   Moon Sign Aquarius

It might now occur to you that you are in a good position to streamline your life in some way. Use today to make changes, in particular ones that involve getting rid of some of the deadwood that is accumulating in your life. Some Taureans may now feel a greater than usual desire to travel.

5 TUESDAY *Moon Age Day 29 Moon Sign Aquarius*

It might feel as if someone is giving you the run around today. The luckiest amongst you will be those who have decided to take a break of some sort at this time. The instinct to mix with many people is strong, as is the general level of enjoyment derived from changing routines and inviting new schedules into your life.

6 WEDNESDAY ☿ *Moon Age Day 0 Moon Sign Pisces*

One-to-one relationships ought to be stimulating today and they offer you an escape from the less flexible qualities of Taurus that have been showing of late. In a general sense you will feel as though you need diversion; this is a hangover of recent planetary trends that haven't been all that useful but which are now changing.

7 THURSDAY ☿ *Moon Age Day 1 Moon Sign Pisces*

Personal relationships should feel more stable now and offer you the chance to retreat a little from the practical aspects of your life and into the bosom of your family. When you are dealing with people beyond your usual circle, it would be best not to draw attention to your own limitations.

8 FRIDAY ☿ *Moon Age Day 2 Moon Sign Aries*

A matter close to your heart takes up a good amount of your time and might slow down your success rate in a number of other situations. It is possible that you are worrying about things unnecessarily and it might be an idea to seek out the help and support of a family member or perhaps a really good friend.

9 SATURDAY ☿ *Moon Age Day 3 Moon Sign Aries*

There should be plenty to smile about at present, especially when it comes to family matters. Even in relationships with those you don't know especially well you should discover some shared interests or viewpoints that bring warmth to these encounters. You are able to understand what friends are asking of you, even when they are virtually silent.

10 SUNDAY ☿ *Moon Age Day 4   Moon Sign Taurus*

An unexpected favour may come your way today under trends which favour good luck all round for you. While it is certainly true that you can gain in all sorts of ways at the moment, more important still is the general popularity that also comes as a result of these planetary positions. At work and at home you seem to be everyone's number one at present.

11 MONDAY ☿ *Moon Age Day 5   Moon Sign Taurus*

This would be a good time to put fresh ideas to the test and to show anyone who has doubted just what you are capable of. Results will almost certainly come along quicker than you might have expected and there are gains to be made from simply being yourself. Comfort and security are out of the window for now and progress is king.

12 TUESDAY ☿ *Moon Age Day 6   Moon Sign Taurus*

Your domestic partner might prove to you just how much they care by making a general fuss of you today. Although you will appreciate their efforts, you are turning your mind more towards the outside world and less to your home. If you think about it, though, there will be ways in which you can mix business and pleasure.

13 WEDNESDAY ☿ *Moon Age Day 7   Moon Sign Gemini*

You will take great pleasure in being on the move at the moment. There is no shortage of opportunities for your fertile mind. Flexible, interested and very friendly, you should surge through the day. If not everything turns out exactly as you would have liked, consider the possibility that perhaps you are simply not trying hard enough.

14 THURSDAY ☿ *Moon Age Day 8   Moon Sign Gemini*

This is potentially a time of small, but regular increases where finances are concerned. Concentrate your effort in places and situations you know and understand. You should be keen to make your willingness to help others known, especially to friends you recognise to be going through a hard time at the moment.

15 FRIDAY ☿ *Moon Age Day 9   Moon Sign Cancer*

There could be love interest on the horizon for Taurus, particularly for those who have been looking for that very special romance. Don't be too quick to jump to conclusions regarding material matters and if you are in any doubt whatsoever about any decision, opt for a patient attitude and bide your time.

16 SATURDAY ☿ *Moon Age Day 10   Moon Sign Cancer*

It would be a good idea to vary your routines just as much as possible this weekend, without planning anything too much. If you remain flexible, it looks likely that all sorts of possibilities will find their way to your door. People you haven't seen for some time could also be turning up on your doorstep soon.

17 SUNDAY ☿ *Moon Age Day 11   Moon Sign Cancer*

Avoid getting carried away with issues that don't have anything directly to do with your life at present. Retain your energy for really important tasks because although you have plenty of get up and go right now, it is easily dissipated. It's quality, rather than quantity that really pays at this time.

18 MONDAY ☿ *Moon Age Day 12   Moon Sign Leo*

Your present mood and the way you project your personality means that you should be able to attract new people into your life now. Although there is a definite shy side to your nature, it doesn't show all that much at present. Most Taureans will be feeling young-at-heart, no matter what their age might be. Go for fun, because that's the most important factor now.

19 TUESDAY ☿ *Moon Age Day 13   Moon Sign Leo*

Mundane and domestic matters can be trying, which is why you are looking for diversity today. Your confidence remains generally high, though there are people around who would change that situation if they could. Watch out for someone who wants to throw a spanner in the works and have faith in your own abilities.

20 WEDNESDAY ☿   *Moon Age Day 14   Moon Sign Virgo*

This looks likely to be a genuinely light-hearted period during which you find the answers you need almost without trying. If you do come up against the odd problem today, there is likely to be someone around who will solve it for you. The difference now is that you are not too shy or retiring to ask.

21 THURSDAY ☿   *Moon Age Day 15   Moon Sign Virgo*

If you turn your attention more today towards the professional side of life, the wonderful array of different planetary positions will help you to make progress today. Mars in its present position is all about efficiency and dealing with matters as and when they arise. There isn't any reason to rush anything and plenty of assistance is on hand.

22 FRIDAY ☿   *Moon Age Day 16   Moon Sign Libra*

Certain people, most likely the ones with whom you work, could be about to test your patience sorely today. For this reason alone, the focus of life should be pushed towards home, family and friendship. Assume for now that work is something you have to do, while your greatest pleasures lie temporarily elsewhere.

23 SATURDAY ☿   *Moon Age Day 17   Moon Sign Libra*

Both socially and romantically, there is much to capture your interest now. It is possible that you are well ahead in your work, which ought to leave time for simply enjoying yourself. Taureans are generally happy when they are consolidating matters and organising their lives – but that is hardly likely to be of much interest during such a spontaneous phase.

24 SUNDAY ☿   *Moon Age Day 18   Moon Sign Scorpio*

Some setbacks appear to be unavoidable today. The lunar low makes you less able to push through obstacles and as a result you feel stuck. The best way to deal with this sort of situation is to tell yourself that in a couple of days the flexible attitude will begin to return and that in the meantime you can do some planning.

25 MONDAY ☿ *Moon Age Day 19 Moon Sign Scorpio*

The lunar low still prevents you from pushing forward with any real dynamism and it seems likely that you will find major plans foundering if you try too hard. Everyone needs to recharge their batteries from time to time and it appears that this is what you are about for the moment. By tomorrow things should be improved.

26 TUESDAY ☿ *Moon Age Day 20 Moon Sign Sagittarius*

Quick thinking and a general mental sharpness typify your nature at present. Mercury is working well for you, inclining you to speak your mind in all situations. Some Taureans will have begun a health kick at the beginning of the year and if this is you, you should see the results beginning to show now.

27 WEDNESDAY ☿ *Moon Age Day 21 Moon Sign Sagittarius*

In a social sense, you should find plenty of light-hearted moments to pep up today, although work-wise you are not in such a good position. It is possible that colleagues will misunderstand your point of view and likewise teachers if you are in further education. Explaining yourself is vital at this time.

28 THURSDAY ☿ *Moon Age Day 22 Moon Sign Capricorn*

Nothing ventured, nothing gained should be your adage now. Yours is not a zodiac sign that is used to taking too many chances, but if you don't do so now, you could be the loser. If you have any doubts, seek out the help and advice of a good friend, someone who will point you in the right direction.

29 FRIDAY *Moon Age Day 23 Moon Sign Capricorn*

Intimate concerns and domestic situations seem to be your most important priorities around now. At what is probably the end of a working week you might be feeling a little unhappy with the general progress you have made, while the underlying truth is that you have done much better overall than you realise.

30 SATURDAY   *Moon Age Day 24   Moon Sign Capricorn*

If you are expecting a great deal of peace and quiet this weekend you might be sorely disappointed. That doesn't mean there is anything negative about today. On the contrary, there is a great deal of enjoyment in store. The only proviso is that you have to let go in order to find and appreciate it.

31 SUNDAY   *Moon Age Day 25   Moon Sign Aquarius*

You are still likely to be getting the best from most spheres of life, though the accent is turning towards domestic matters. Relatives may have special need of you today and you should certainly be willing to help out when you can. Real puzzles are something you might want to mull over for a while.

8
April
2019

1 MONDAY
Moon Age Day 26   Moon Sign Aquarius

A professional issue could cause a rather tense atmosphere today unless you take it by the scruff of the neck and deal with it immediately. You need to be very direct in all your dealings right now because hedging your bets work under current trends. Friends may display a disquieting lack of confidence in you.

2 TUESDAY
Moon Age Day 27   Moon Sign Pisces

It seems likely that you will enjoy being the centre of attention wherever you go today. It would be a shame if the planetary aspects creating this tendency were wasted simply because this was nothing more than a routine day. Put yourself out to make sure there are social possibilities after work.

3 WEDNESDAY
Moon Age Day 28   Moon Sign Pisces

You know the value of self-reliance and are usually happy to go your own way. This is particularly true today. Your strength of personality is rock solid, causing others to have a deep and abiding confidence in your decisions. The fact that this appears to place an extra burden on you is something you don't recognise at all.

4 THURSDAY
Moon Age Day 29   Moon Sign Pisces

You take professional issues in your stride and are happy to prove once again how reliable you are, even when under a small amount of stress. You can't expect everyone to agree with your point of view at the moment but in this instance, the planets suggest that you could turn out to be right. Try to get your point across if you can.

5 FRIDAY
Moon Age Day 0   Moon Sign Aries

This is a good day to be around the people you care for the most. Although you have been sociable and stepped out of your comfort zone on quite a few occasions recently, in the main you are happiest when you understand your surroundings and the people within it. Still, one or two friends prove to be positively inspirational.

6 SATURDAY
Moon Age Day 1   Moon Sign Aries

Having fun is likely to be your number one priority this Saturday. Although this may be somewhat difficult in the middle of a busy life, you do presently have the ability to mix business with pleasure and to enjoy them both. Look for people who haven't been around recently and take the chance to have a chat.

7 SUNDAY
Moon Age Day 2   Moon Sign Taurus

Almost anything you have planned for today should go well, mainly due to the level of effort you are willing and able to put in. A strong surge of good luck may attend much of what you do, making this a perfect time to back your hunches all the way when it comes to relationships and plans.

8 MONDAY
Moon Age Day 3   Moon Sign Taurus

There are now great opportunities to make gains and you will not want to let these pass you by. Shopping today could lead to the discovery of genuine bargains, whilst social possibilities look particularly good. If there isn't much happening around you, the chances are you are not trying hard enough.

9 TUESDAY
Moon Age Day 4   Moon Sign Gemini

Prepare for some minor mishaps today, though most of them can presently be viewed in a humorous way. It is hard to take anything particularly seriously now as all you really want is to have fun. The practical joker within you now shines out, and you are more than happy to put it to good use! Take care that the recipient of your joke will see the funny side, though.

10 WEDNESDAY   *Moon Age Day 5   Moon Sign Gemini*

Part of today could be spent coming to terms with a personal issue. Have confidence in your dealings with others and avoid giving anyone the impression that you are not sure of yourself regarding decisions you wish to take. Friends should prove to be especially helpful at the moment and genuinely keen to lend a hand.

11 THURSDAY   *Moon Age Day 6   Moon Sign Gemini*

It is towards the practical aspects of life that your mind now turns. You might discover a number of new ways to get ahead with your work and should also be enjoying the cut and thrust of an active life that could involve colleagues. Family matters might have to be left on the backburner for a short while.

12 FRIDAY   *Moon Age Day 7   Moon Sign Cancer*

Where decisions and methods are concerned today, you will show rather more circumspection than was the case yesterday. Now the innate caution that is part of your zodiac sign reveals itself, leading you to proceed with caution. Any disputes still around in friendship circles can therefore be quickly cleared up.

13 SATURDAY   *Moon Age Day 8   Moon Sign Cancer*

A financial issue is apt to prove somewhat complicated, leading you to seek the advice of someone who is more in the know than you are. Don't avoid discussions simply because you are not in a chatty frame of mind, things need sorting out and you won't manage that without talking.

14 SUNDAY   *Moon Age Day 9   Moon Sign Leo*

Get ready to take a starring role today. Planetary trends are lining up once again to offer you a great deal of incentive. Although your practical progress could be marred because this is Sunday, you are having no difficulty whatsoever in making valuable allies. New friendships are likely to be formed at this time.

15 MONDAY
Moon Age Day 10   Moon Sign Leo

The planets place a very strong emphasis on the fun side of life and it is possible that you find it difficult to take certain matters seriously. You might have to pretend that you do, though only for the sake of those around you. Give yourself a pat on the back for a recent success that looks likely to lead to more.

16 TUESDAY
Moon Age Day 11   Moon Sign Virgo

Warring factions amongst family and friends may address the sort of issues that you feel need attention, and might also allow you to show that you have your practical head on at present. Smoothing over disagreements could be easy for you today, not least of all because Taurus is a natural peacemaker in any case.

17 WEDNESDAY
Moon Age Day 12   Moon Sign Virgo

Better by far today to take life steadily and to make sure that you have your facts right, no matter what you undertake. Routines are not difficult to deal with at this stage though not everyone is going to be quite as helpful as you might hope, especially when it comes to your work. It would be sensible to check and recheck most details if you want to make sure you are on the right path.

18 THURSDAY
Moon Age Day 13   Moon Sign Libra

In certain situations others may expect you to step down and that's something that is difficult for the average Taurean to do. It has to be said, though, that a little flexibility at this stage could see you reaping greater benefits further down the line. When it comes to speaking words of love, you won't have any problems today.

19 FRIDAY
Moon Age Day 14   Moon Sign Libra

Getting on with what is necessary can be something of a chore and it is quite possible that you will decide to alter your routines as a result. Not everyone finds this easy to come to terms with but those you really care about will co-operate. It should not be difficult to get others to follow your lead under present astrological trends.

20 SATURDAY   *Moon Age Day 15   Moon Sign Scorpio*

The lunar low is almost certain to slow things down, though not disproportionately. All you really notice this time around is the fact that things are not going exactly your way. If you stay away from material considerations and concentrate on having fun, the position of the Moon won't affect you at all.

21 SUNDAY   *Moon Age Day 16   Moon Sign Scorpio*

There are some tests of your patience to be dealt with today, but the same rules as yesterday still apply. Family matters are easy to deal with but you could find a certain restless streak beginning to develop within you. Go for anything that feels different, but stay away from undue risks for the moment.

22 MONDAY   *Moon Age Day 17   Moon Sign Sagittarius*

Trends indicate a professional boost at the beginning of this week. The help and support of colleagues could prove to be extremely important and it seems there could be some extra help from some unexpected directions. It also seems likely that some close personal contacts might have some news to impart.

23 TUESDAY   *Moon Age Day 18   Moon Sign Sagittarius*

This would be a very good day for collecting and collating any sort of information, some of which may prove to be very important later. You will be more than ready to move ahead quickly with important matters and actively want to get involved in situations you could well have shied away from previously.

24 WEDNESDAY   *Moon Age Day 19   Moon Sign Capricorn*

Your constant desire to keep life on an even keel could be somewhat upset by the foolish actions of others. Ignore this if you can and opt for a positive day with plenty of social contact and a continued determination to break through barriers. Stay away from negative people who only have doom and gloom to impart.

25 THURSDAY   *Moon Age Day 20   Moon Sign Capricorn*

It isn't hard for you to get on with anyone right now and you will have a particular fondness for those who can be termed 'real characters'. Such individuals bring out the slightly quirky side of your own nature and stop you from becoming serious about anything. What you most want from today is a laugh.

26 FRIDAY   *Moon Age Day 21   Moon Sign Capricorn*

Approaching life today with the sort of abandon that can occasionally be missing from the Taurean life, you are now very entertaining to have around. Of course there is the chance you will say something that will cause you embarrassment later – but what does that matter? The Bull is in full swing and everyone wants to hear you.

27 SATURDAY   *Moon Age Day 22   Moon Sign Aquarius*

Contributing to your own success isn't hard today and whatever happens you should feel in charge of situations. If this really does not seem to be possible you must rely on trust, even if this is sometimes difficult for you. Taurus does invariably want to run the entire show but sometimes needs to recognise that this can't happen.

28 SUNDAY   *Moon Age Day 23   Moon Sign Aquarius*

Your concentration probably isn't all it should be at the moment. If you know that this is the case then right from the start you need to ask someone to remind you of particular jobs you have to do. Although you will not want to rely on others, you could find you make new friends. Don't be afraid to trust someone today.

29 MONDAY   *Moon Age Day 24   Moon Sign Pisces*

You will probably spend at least part of today with special friends. These are the people who are not afraid to tell you the truth. Of course you don't always relish their words, but you do know why they say the things they do. Getting close to people is much easier for you now than would usually be the case, even for Taurus.

30 TUESDAY

Moon Age Day 25   Moon Sign Pisces

If you are between jobs or retired this could be a good period for taking on some new project that you simply find interesting. Look out for romance, which shows itself at almost any stage between now and the middle of next week. In a professional sense you might have to repeat jobs a number of times today.

2019

1 WEDNESDAY *Moon Age Day 26   Moon Sign Pisces*

This could turn out to be a taxing time at work, so you should be grateful once the responsibility is out of the way and you can finally please yourself. Socially, you are on top form, which may be one of the reasons you are less professionally inclined at the moment.

2 THURSDAY *Moon Age Day 27   Moon Sign Aries*

This is one of the best days of this month to enjoy some personal freedom, so much so that if you are not able to do this you could end up feeling hemmed in by circumstances. Try to break down any barriers in your way if you can. Stay mobile and give your full attention to any situation that stimulates your mind.

3 FRIDAY *Moon Age Day 28   Moon Sign Aries*

This is not a day during which you should be too worried about completing tasks. It would be better right now to make sure you are doing things properly, even if they take more time than usual. The best way to get what you want from life is to concentrate on whatever tasks you are addressing.

4 SATURDAY *Moon Age Day 0   Moon Sign Taurus*

The lunar high finds you perfectly placed to make real headway in a number of different areas of life. Not only are you working well in a professional sense, you are also thinking about taking up new interests, probably alongside people you like a great deal. Avoid unnecessary confrontations at present.

5 SUNDAY
Moon Age Day 1   Moon Sign Taurus

The more time you can apportion to your own plans today, the better things will go. Try to put routine tasks aside and strike out towards your personal ambitions whenever you can. You can expect to get a lot done during this active weekend and should be well placed to make advances in friendship and romance.

6 MONDAY
Moon Age Day 2   Moon Sign Taurus

Any outdoor pursuit should be appealing to you now. As summer approaches, the stronger your urge is to be out of doors and active. Be led by your own ideas about how to have fun, but do it in the company of people you find amusing, educating and charming.

7 TUESDAY
Moon Age Day 3   Moon Sign Gemini

Your communicative skills look set to be strong at the moment and what sets the rest of this week apart is your skill in getting others to understand your point of view. Generally cheerful, you are good to have around and most of the people you know will be pleased to have you on board in any situation.

8 WEDNESDAY
Moon Age Day 4   Moon Sign Gemini

While it may be easy to get along with others at work today, things may not be quite so rosy in a personal or romantic sense. It appears you are not able to tell people quite the way you feel, leading to misunderstandings and even disputes. Of course, it takes two to tango so actively make the choice to keep out of any conflict.

9 THURSDAY
Moon Age Day 5   Moon Sign Cancer

Your good mood and sparkling personality are most obvious in the way you are happy to talk to anyone about almost any topic. So exuberant are you at present that it will be difficult for others to get a word in edgeways. It is unlikely that they will object, however, because you are so good to have around now.

10 FRIDAY *Moon Age Day 6   Moon Sign Cancer*

You think deeply and in a very capable manner today. This fact is not lost on others, who should be only too willing to seek your advice on a number of different topics. Try to stay active because long periods sitting and doing very little won't suit you, either in a mental or a physical way.

11 SATURDAY *Moon Age Day 7   Moon Sign Leo*

Your love life and romantic matters in general show a definite improvement with the arrival of the weekend. This may be partly due to the fact that you have more time to concentrate on the needs of those around you, particularly your partner. Don't be too quick to volunteer for jobs around the home, however, because they can mount up.

12 SUNDAY *Moon Age Day 8   Moon Sign Leo*

A good time on the home front could help to alleviate the small problems now cropping up in other spheres of your life, particularly at work. Personal relationships ought to work rather well and offer you the chance to say things that might have been on your mind for quite some time.

13 MONDAY *Moon Age Day 9   Moon Sign Virgo*

Trends move on and it is now your professional life that is most rewarding, although good news is likely to be on the way that might also have a bearing on your romantic interests. Hold tight to money for the moment because the best bargains come along later this month. In the meantime take care with your spending.

14 TUESDAY *Moon Age Day 10   Moon Sign Virgo*

Your opinions may get you quite fired up at present, tending to make you rather emphatic in discussions. Be just a little careful because it is possible to cause offence without intending to do so. This is especially true if you are dealing with sensitive people who don't quite know how you take your present attitude.

15 WEDNESDAY   *Moon Age Day 11   Moon Sign Libra*

The seesaw that is life is in operation again, bringing with it a short period during which the charm you have been showing of late takes something of a holiday. You may have to work hard today to accommodate those you really don't like, and to disguise the fact from both them and yourself.

16 THURSDAY   *Moon Age Day 12   Moon Sign Libra*

For the first time in a while you could find yourself at odds with others in specific situations. This need not be a curse, but it really depends on the way you deal with the situation. It's quite important to keep your cool and to realise that certain short-term astrological trends are not working with you.

17 FRIDAY   *Moon Age Day 13   Moon Sign Scorpio*

Your professional progress is slowed markedly as the lunar low pays its monthly visit. Fortunately, there are some strong planetary trends in evidence so the power of the Moon's influence is somewhat diminished this time around. In a social and romantic sense, you may barely notice the difference.

18 SATURDAY   *Moon Age Day 14   Moon Sign Scorpio*

Your judgement is apt to be slightly marred today and you can't get as much from situations as you might wish. Be patient because the present trends are not long lasting and tomorrow will bring a very different story. What might be frustrating at present is the fact that nobody seems willing to listen to you.

19 SUNDAY   *Moon Age Day 15   Moon Sign Scorpio*

You want to get away from mundane issues during Sunday and won't be all that keen to sit around at home, no matter how appealing that might have seemed early in the working week. There is a desire for fresh fields and pastures new, which is as much a response to the season as to any astrological trend.

20 MONDAY · *Moon Age Day 16 · Moon Sign Sagittarius*

One-to-one relationships could be the source of some bickering today, though this is completely pointless and you would do yourself a real favour if you refused to become involved. Relationships where you have less emotional involvement, such as those with friends or colleagues, might be safer.

21 TUESDAY · *Moon Age Day 17 · Moon Sign Sagittarius*

Professional progress continues to come easily and might well be the area of life you choose to concentrate on now. The attitude of most people with whom you are making contact is fair and getting them to listen to your present, unique point of view is likely to be easier than you might think.

22 WEDNESDAY · *Moon Age Day 18 · Moon Sign Capricorn*

There is good progress to be made just as long as you stay out there in the big, wide world. This is no time to be hiding your light under a bushel because people want to see you exactly as you are. It wouldn't be fair to say fame and fortune await you today, but you could at least enjoy what is on offer.

23 THURSDAY · *Moon Age Day 19 · Moon Sign Capricorn*

You may now get an opportunity to broaden your horizons, probably as a result of new activities or travel. The time is right to opt for a little culture and the more intelligent qualities of your birth sign are definitely on display. Don't be held back by the negative thinking of just one person.

24 FRIDAY · *Moon Age Day 20 · Moon Sign Aquarius*

Prepare for some minor frustrations at this time, though if you are prepared for them they should not pose too much of a problem. These will undoubtedly come from the direction of close friends or family members, some of whom are unwilling or unable to follow your present reasoning and so could cause delays.

25 SATURDAY   *Moon Age Day 21   Moon Sign Aquarius*

Others find it easy to make contact with you now and the more chatty side of Taurus is definitely on display. For the last few days some Taureans have been showing the slightly more withdrawn side of their nature. Now you can shine and see your popularity increase as a result.

26 SUNDAY   *Moon Age Day 22   Moon Sign Aquarius*

Pressures can arise at home and a loved one might need more tolerance and understanding as a result. In some ways you are torn because at the same time what is on offer out there in the wider world is also quite appealing. Some way or another you are going to have to compartmentalise your time.

27 MONDAY   *Moon Age Day 23   Moon Sign Pisces*

Others now find your ideas particularly interesting and will actively support what you are saying. However, beware of a slight tendency to be distracted, especially by matters that look intriguing but which might have no practical application. Being interested is fine but this is a time for genuine progress.

28 TUESDAY   *Moon Age Day 24   Moon Sign Pisces*

Where professional issues are concerned you find yourself well in the know and seeking out some sort of advancement. It might be that you are being told what to do by people you consider less qualified than you are. However, a degree of co-operation with them will work far better than direct criticism.

29 WEDNESDAY   *Moon Age Day 25   Moon Sign Aries*

You won't have any real trouble discovering where interesting things are happening, or assessing who holds the most useful information in any situation. This is certainly a period during which you benefit from keeping on the move. The old stick-in-the-mud that Taurus can be on occasions is nowhere to be seen at this stage of the month.

30 THURSDAY
Moon Age Day 26   Moon Sign Aries

There can be minor social disappointments today, possibly because you are expecting rather too much of one or two specific people. Spread your time and your interests as much as you can right now and don't be too specific in your objectives. Not everyone proves to be as reliable as you might wish.

31 FRIDAY
Moon Age Day 27   Moon Sign Aries

You will undoubtedly be in a restless frame of mind right now and keen to try out some new proposals. If you are a working Taurus, there is room for advancement now or at the very least a promise of it in the not too distant future. Concentrating on matters that don't interest you is likely to be difficult.

2019

1 SATURDAY
Moon Age Day 28   Moon Sign Taurus

The lunar high this month has some very practical applications, which suit you down to the ground. Your sphere of influence is strong, both at work and at home. Changes you have wanted to implement for some time now become entirely possible, and the more so if you show yourself to be dynamic.

2 SUNDAY
Moon Age Day 29   Moon Sign Taurus

This is a bonus period for personal relationships and for love especially. Showing your partner or sweetheart how you feel about them isn't at all difficult. Since the lunar high invariably brings better-than-average luck, it is also fair to suggest that you can take a little chance in some way today.

3 MONDAY
Moon Age Day 0   Moon Sign Gemini

Expect a few ups and downs in finances today. Be prepared to adapt to outside circumstances and also possibly to recognise a few limitations that are likely to be placed upon you now. In terms of personal relationships, this week should prove to be secure and see a deepening of affection.

4 TUESDAY
Moon Age Day 1   Moon Sign Gemini

This is a day for enjoying the social whirl and for communicating your ideas to others. You may need a bit more mental focus because you may not be seeing all situations the way they really are. However, your confidence in your own abilities is on the increase and you might take a chance today that you wouldn't have considered earlier on in the year.

5 WEDNESDAY *Moon Age Day 2   Moon Sign Cancer*

You won't have to try very hard to impress anyone at the moment. All the same, compromise is a word you do need to keep in mind and there is no gain at all now from refusing to adapt, even though your instincts tell you otherwise. Impulsive actions are not as likely to bring rewards as well-thought-out ones.

6 THURSDAY *Moon Age Day 3   Moon Sign Cancer*

The planets put you in a go-ahead mood and help you to latch on to any practical advantage that is around at the moment. Your confidence continues to grow, though the later part of this week may bring some small reversals. In a general sense, your life is moving forward, even if your progress is steady at present.

7 FRIDAY *Moon Age Day 4   Moon Sign Leo*

A boost comes along as far as your social life is concerned. Together with others, you will find this an interesting time once the concerns of the material world have been dealt with. You could also notice an upturn in general fortune and financial strength beginning any time now.

8 SATURDAY *Moon Age Day 5   Moon Sign Leo*

Your partner could now play a more dominant role in your life, but only because that is the way you want the situation to be. In other spheres, you need to look very carefully at suggestions that are being made which somehow have a bearing on your working circumstances. Perhaps negotiation is necessary.

9 SUNDAY *Moon Age Day 6   Moon Sign Virgo*

This particular Sunday coincides with trends that particularly favour co-operative ventures of any sort. Be willing to put yourself out for the sake of the group as a whole, whilst continuing to plough your own furrow in other ways. What you shouldn't do today is to find yourself completely out on a limb.

10 MONDAY
Moon Age Day 7   Moon Sign Virgo

What you tend to deal with at the start of this working week is long-term plans and the strategies necessary to get what you want from your working life. Don't be too quick to jump to conclusions where the apparent actions of others are concerned. Give situations time to mature.

11 TUESDAY
Moon Age Day 8   Moon Sign Virgo

You want to be in charge of finances now, even though others could disagree. What you must do is to put forward a reasoned argument, explaining your point of view. If that doesn't work, leave things alone for a day or two. You should leave some time today to talk about less serious matters and to have fun.

12 WEDNESDAY
Moon Age Day 9   Moon Sign Libra

Things that happen today could enhance your career prospects no end. You need to keep your eyes open because there are some helpful people and situations around. If you are presently engaged on a health kick of some sort, just remember that success comes through methodical application, not sudden changes.

13 THURSDAY
Moon Age Day 10   Moon Sign Libra

It is likely that the things people say today boost your ego and your confidence. If you feel that your week has so far not been the best, take heart from the fact that there are better things in store. Taurus may be in a thoughtful mood today and so you could find yourself rather less physically active.

14 FRIDAY
Moon Age Day 11   Moon Sign Scorpio

Avoid taking risks in any ongoing situation. The lunar low could lead you to feel that some of the advantages you have built for yourself in the last week or two are in danger, so you need to exercise extra care today. Emotionally speaking, you are likely to feel stronger and generally more resilient.

15 SATURDAY   *Moon Age Day 12   Moon Sign Scorpio*

The lunar low is still present, but there are also progressive trends in your chart, especially those dealing with social occasions and leisure. You might be slightly restricted in a material sense, but that won't prevent you from finding enjoyment. However, you will probably feel more comfortable within your family.

16 SUNDAY   *Moon Age Day 13   Moon Sign Sagittarius*

You easily express charm, grace and harmony at the moment, so it is no wonder that you are wowing almost everyone you come across. This would be a good time to concentrate on love and also to make a startling impression on people who can have an important part to play in your life in the months to come.

17 MONDAY   *Moon Age Day 14   Moon Sign Sagittarius*

Romantic and social activity tends to be happy and harmonious around this time. There could be one or two surprises in the offing, plus the chance to get something that you have wanted for quite some time. It will be necessary to see one or two jobs through to completion if you really want to profit now.

18 TUESDAY   *Moon Age Day 15   Moon Sign Capricorn*

Things are likely to be rather hectic today and there won't be too much time to catch your breath. To a great extent you have to rely on your intuition and upon the advice of specific people who you know to have your best interests at heart. Look out for very rewarding situations at work, mainly because of the effort you put in.

19 WEDNESDAY   *Moon Age Day 16   Moon Sign Capricorn*

If you want assistance for personal efforts, you will have the necessary cheek to ask for it today. Few aspects of life are working against your best interests right now and in some ways you find this to be an important turning point generally. Although changes look like being low-key, they should be very significant in the end.

20 THURSDAY   *Moon Age Day 17   Moon Sign Capricorn*

There is now likely to be some hopeful news arriving regarding situations that might not appear to have been working out well for you recently. There is plenty of room for romance in your life at present and it appears that you are taking the time to show your partner, or someone you really like, how very kind you can be.

21 FRIDAY   *Moon Age Day 18   Moon Sign Aquarius*

Relationships may offer the best way forward today, as would a shopping excursion or perhaps a social event of some sort. The planetary picture favours time spent with friends, though you have it within you to mix business with pleasure at the moment and can easily make profit from what seems a purely personal event.

22 SATURDAY   *Moon Age Day 19   Moon Sign Aquarius*

A more than favourable period is coming along now, especially with regard to relationships, which look particularly settled around this time. Whether in business or pleasure, twosomes work especially well for you and co-operative ventures of any sort now look likely to turn out well.

23 SUNDAY   *Moon Age Day 20   Moon Sign Pisces*

You will almost certainly have good ideas for improving situations at work, even if Sunday is a day of rest as far as you are concerned. In between finding excellent ways to enjoy yourself, it is clear that you are casting your mind into the future and coming up with some cracking schemes.

24 MONDAY   *Moon Age Day 21   Moon Sign Pisces*

You ought to find yourself in amongst just the right company today and can make the most positive of impressions when it really counts. Your social and love lives are likely to be especially fulfilling around now and you won't have any problem at all getting others to join in the fun you are instigating.

25 TUESDAY
Moon Age Day 22   Moon Sign Pisces

The ability to get along well and easily with others is now very strong indeed. Although you may not be letting your hair down big-time, and might be showing some caution, you have powerful social inclinations now and want to share your opinions with others. A short journey might suit you well.

26 WEDNESDAY
Moon Age Day 23   Moon Sign Aries

Look out for some new ideas that should be coming along at any time now. You know what you want from life today and in general it shouldn't be difficult to get it. Showing concern for those in trouble is pretty much what you are about as a person and this really does show between now and the weekend.

27 THURSDAY
Moon Age Day 24   Moon Sign Aries

When it comes to looking after your own interests, you are second to none. This is particularly true in the financial sphere and with regard to work. Don't be at all surprised if a number of quite significant invitations are coming your way during the next couple of days. Your popularity is more or less assured.

28 FRIDAY
Moon Age Day 25   Moon Sign Taurus

The lunar high is likely to herald a far better period on the financial front. Maybe you are about to back some scheme or enterprise that has been important to you for a while? You take a sensible view of things and you can also rely on the very positive support that seems to be coming from colleagues and your partner.

29 SATURDAY
Moon Age Day 26   Moon Sign Taurus

The second day of the lunar high finds you still able to get ahead. Be prepared to make decisions and don't be worried if it appears that you are being put on the spot. Concern for those who are less well off than you is uppermost in your mind at all times now and you show yourself to be a true friend.

30 SUNDAY   *Moon Age Day 27   Moon Sign Gemini*

Mixing freely with your friends this Sunday, you could discover that one or two of them hold a key that can open some very interesting doors for you. Because you are now so open-minded, you will be looking at matters you probably avoided before and can find yourself entering a very interesting and quite unusual phase in your life.

2019

1 MONDAY
Moon Age Day 28   Moon Sign Gemini

You might find yourself compelled to go over the ins and outs of an emotional matter today, something that you would probably avoid altogether if you could. Don't be too quick to judge either the motives or actions of another person, just in case you find yourself facing the same situation some day.

2 TUESDAY
Moon Age Day 0   Moon Sign Gemini

There should be much happening in personal relationships that will make you feel quite joyful. You could do worse than to get intimate with someone you really care about and there probably hasn't been a better time this year for Taurus when it comes to new love blossoming and growing apace.

3 WEDNESDAY
Moon Age Day 1   Moon Sign Cancer

Although you will be quite restless at present, this need not be a bad thing. Rather than sitting around in a jittery state, you need to harness the trend and make it work for you constructively. Any mind-broadening experience can be considered and once again you may have a strong desire to do some travelling.

4 THURSDAY
Moon Age Day 2   Moon Sign Cancer

Getting out of doors seems really appealing to you at present, and the warmth of the summer breezes also encourages you to look beyond your own immediate vicinity for new experiences. Any change you make at the moment will do you good but you might have to settle one or two issues at home first.

5 FRIDAY
Moon Age Day 3   Moon Sign Leo

You might be in for one or two slightly unpleasant experiences if you put your trust in the wrong sort of people right now. Use your intuition and your Taurean, Earth-sign common sense when assessing anything. If you are involved in any sort of sporting activity, now is the time to go for gold and to win.

6 SATURDAY
Moon Age Day 4   Moon Sign Leo

A continued interest in what makes the world tick can set this Saturday apart, though quite a few Taureans will find themselves to be in relaxation mode. There are many changes to come with the new week and directly conflicting interests to be dealt with. If things are peaceful now, enjoy the break.

7 SUNDAY
Moon Age Day 5   Moon Sign Virgo

Your social life and relationships are now under the spotlight and might be found wanting in some way. Certainly you are likely to make far-reaching changes, either now or soon and it is likely that these will leave you with more time to enjoy the company of people you like a great deal.

8 MONDAY
☿   *Moon Age Day 6   Moon Sign Virgo*

You would be well advised to abandon whatever isn't working and to concentrate instead on a few simple strategies. Your confidence to do the right thing remains generally high and you won't be easily distracted from the task at hand. Although it might be easy to submit to pressure today, you are unlikely to do so.

9 TUESDAY
☿   *Moon Age Day 7   Moon Sign Libra*

You are now caught up in a swiftly moving period with aspects of your life changing quite rapidly. Don't be fooled into thinking that someone you might mix with professionally knows better than you do how to run your life. The fact is that only you have the most intimate understanding of the way things truly are.

10 WEDNESDAY ☿   *Moon Age Day 8   Moon Sign Libra*

Your sense of adventure definitely increases and you now have more contact with quite cultured types. The trends at the moment are excellent for travel and for broadening your mind, and the position of Venus especially makes you behave in a way that lets others know just how highbrow you can be when you put your mind to it.

11 THURSDAY ☿   *Moon Age Day 9   Moon Sign Scorpio*

If any major decisions are required on a personal level today, allow your partner to handle them. For your part, you should be more than happy to take a break and to decide later how problems should be addressed. If you spend time at home and relax, you may not even notice that the lunar low has brought you any constraints at all.

12 FRIDAY ☿   *Moon Age Day 10   Moon Sign Scorpio*

Once the afternoon comes along today, your dealings with others should prove to be happy and full of positivity. Don't make any major changes before lunchtime and count to ten before you speak. Later in the day some positive planetary trends take over and then it's happiness all the way.

13 SATURDAY ☿ *Moon Age Day 11   Moon Sign Sagittarius*

Though you are probably thinking big, and maybe acting quite big too, deep inside you are not nearly as sure of yourself as you like to pretend. It's time to admit your limitations, perhaps to someone you trust. A person you consider either older or wiser than yourself should be more than pleased to listen to what you have to say.

14 SUNDAY ☿ *Moon Age Day 12   Moon Sign Sagittarius*

You enjoy increased concentration and perception, which lifts the possibilities for Sunday no end. Although you can now get on very well in a practical sense, it is the social trends that count the most. A very unusual streak comes along and the Bull is now even more willing to look at long shots and calculated risks.

15 MONDAY ☿ *Moon Age Day 13   Moon Sign Capricorn*

When it comes to money matters, you should find that present planetary influences will be very much more than neutral. That doesn't mean you will be spending lavishly because, in the main, the things you enjoy at the moment are not likely to cost you a penny. Today could so easily be based around friendship.

16 TUESDAY ☿ *Moon Age Day 14   Moon Sign Capricorn*

You can bend career matters your own way and stand a chance of making a good impression on others at the moment. Your confidence is certainly not lacking, though you could also discover that someone you counted as a friend is not doing you any favours. If this is the case, try not to over-react to the situation.

17 WEDNESDAY ☿ *Moon Age Day 15   Moon Sign Capricorn*

This could be a good day for family get-togethers or reunions of some sort. With a slightly nostalgic streak taking over, perhaps you are looking on the internet to see if you can locate some of those buddies you haven't seen for years. If you find them, be prepared for one or two surprises.

18 THURSDAY ☿ *Moon Age Day 16   Moon Sign Aquarius*

This is another of those periods during which you are happy to be in the social spotlight. Taurus is more gregarious at the moment than would usually be the case. Don't panic though, because you still maintain that slight inner reserve that marks you out as being different from the showy zodiac signs.

19 FRIDAY ☿ *Moon Age Day 17   Moon Sign Aquarius*

Some emotional tensions look likely today, perhaps caused by the behaviour of some colleagues. Although you demonstrate great loyalty this month, unfortunately it probably won't always be coming back to you in the way you would wish or expect. Some situations may need you to use your well-honed intuition.

20 SATURDAY ☿ *Moon Age Day 18   Moon Sign Pisces*

The more ambitious you are today, the better you are likely to be getting on. Keep your ears open because even the most casual of conversations could be carrying some surprising but useful news. In any situation, it can be quite crucial to strike while the iron is hot. If you are at work, you are a force to be reckoned with.

21 SUNDAY ☿ *Moon Age Day 19   Moon Sign Pisces*

A fairly cautious approach is necessary now where money is concerned, but the same cannot be said in the realms of romance. Here, Taurus is the king or queen. Almost unconsciously, you heap so many compliments on the object of your desire that they will be putty in your hands.

22 MONDAY ☿ *Moon Age Day 20   Moon Sign Pisces*

Your social life is now your main focus. There are trends around at the moment that would make this period ideal for travel, so maybe a holiday is on the cards? Avoid allowing any of your plans to be too much altered by the attitude and opinions of people who are not really involved in them at all.

23 TUESDAY ☿ *Moon Age Day 21   Moon Sign Aries*

You now find yourself at the start of a go-ahead period and a time during which your progress depends almost entirely on the amount of effort you are willing to put in. You can contribute to little family triumphs around now, but make sure you set aside some moments for quiet contemplation.

24 WEDNESDAY ☿ *Moon Age Day 22   Moon Sign Aries*

You are now in a very good position to influence others. This applies particularly at work. Even if a degree of gentle coercion or encouragement is necessary, as long as you know the end genuinely does justify the means, you should go ahead. Once work is out of the way, you might be especially pleased to be out of doors.

25 THURSDAY ☿ *Moon Age Day 23 Moon Sign Taurus*

Plans that have been up in the air recently now come together and the lunar high brings more potency to your life generally. This is a time to enjoy yourself and to let everyone around you know that you are in command of your own destiny. Shouting your own abilities from the rooftops isn't very Taurus, but it could be useful.

26 FRIDAY ☿ *Moon Age Day 24 Moon Sign Taurus*

Some sort of a gamble could pay off well today, even though you should certainly not be putting your entire fortune on the next race! Your speculations are usually clever and look to be particularly so under present astrological trends. Always use your common sense though, and never bet what you cannot afford to lose. Trends also favour asking someone for what you really want.

27 SATURDAY ☿ *Moon Age Day 25 Moon Sign Taurus*

The most casual of meetings could turn into something much more interesting. Although there are one or two people around now who are not all that trustworthy, it should not be difficult to see through them. The most appealing thing about today is the sheer volume of work you can get through.

28 SUNDAY ☿ *Moon Age Day 26 Moon Sign Gemini*

You have a strong thirst for fresh experiences now. Seeking out change and variety in your life is likely to be extremely important and there are very few difficult trends to deal with right now. Although you are good at problem solving, you might have to seek out an expert during today or tomorrow.

29 MONDAY ☿ *Moon Age Day 27 Moon Sign Gemini*

What really does matter today is the number and quality of contacts you are making. It is for this reason that you can't really afford to put your feet up too much. Action is the key to success, no matter what area of life you are looking at. A strong attachment could be formed as the week gets going.

30 TUESDAY ☿ *Moon Age Day 28 Moon Sign Cancer*

You show considerable charm today, especially in the way you deal with older people, or those people within society who are the most vulnerable. Very philanthropic right now, Taureans may be doing a great deal to raise money, not only in a direct sense, but also in terms of prior planning and new enterprises.

31 WEDNESDAY ☿ *Moon Age Day 0 Moon Sign Cancer*

There is quite a lot of progress to be made today, particularly at work. At the same time, you should be champing at the bit with regard to home-based alterations. With the best of the summer weather still to come it could be that you are altering the shape or composition of your garden. You are very creative at present.

⑧ *August* 2019

1 THURSDAY
Moon Age Day 1   Moon Sign Leo

Partnerships could turn out to be especially lucky at the moment. This may relate to personal attachments, but is just as likely to be professional associations. Set out to have a good time today and talk as much as you can. It's plain that people are listening at the moment and that you are influencing them significantly.

2 FRIDAY
Moon Age Day 2   Moon Sign Leo

Keep a sense of proportion when you have to deal with people who seem determined to be awkward and learn that you can find humour even in the grumpy ways of certain types. There should be a good deal of emphasis on the fun side of life now and the end of this working week offers opportunities for diversion.

3 SATURDAY
Moon Age Day 3   Moon Sign Virgo

Stay away from people who want to complicate situations and take the surest path you can through any job you become involved in. Be prepared for a little romance to enter your life before the day is out. This might turn out to be the case whether you are looking for love or not at the present time.

4 SUNDAY
Moon Age Day 4   Moon Sign Virgo

Try to keep social matters light and enjoyable, whilst at the same time offering a hand to people who are in need of your special brand of help and support. Today is good for discovering alternative types of assistance, some of which is coming from a new direction.

5 MONDAY
Moon Age Day 5   Moon Sign Libra

It is almost certain that emotional ties work better today than casual friendships. For this reason romantically tied Taureans will be actively choosing to spend time with partners. Although there are slight problems around at the moment, with some common sense and a dollop of sound advice, you can get round and through these.

6 TUESDAY
Moon Age Day 6   Moon Sign Libra

Planetary influences that have a bearing on your home life now begin to be felt. It is possible that you will be involved in some family discussions and might also be talking about something important with your partner. If you don't have a romantic partner at the moment, just keep your eyes open.

7 WEDNESDAY
Moon Age Day 7   Moon Sign Scorpio

The present Taurean yearning for adventure and a change of scenery remains undiminished. Get whatever you have to do out of the way and then head for the hills. Even if this proves to be impossible there is nothing at all to prevent your mind from wandering. You should be in a particularly sensitive and caring mood at the moment.

8 THURSDAY
Moon Age Day 8   Moon Sign Scorpio

Professional developments could lead to some moderate gains for you, but the real advances will be made before or after work. Socially speaking, you are on quite a high and enjoying all the attention that comes your way. Avoid any petty jealousy, inside or outside of work.

9 FRIDAY
Moon Age Day 9   Moon Sign Sagittarius

Stay away from the arguments of others because you could so easily be drawn into matters that are nothing to do with you. The more light-hearted you are, the better the day will be. There is something really funny to laugh at right now and if you can't think what it is, maybe you are the one who will be creating the situation.

10 SATURDAY *Moon Age Day 10   Moon Sign Sagittarius*

Avoid being too critical of the way others are behaving because in similar circumstances you might not be able to do any better. Although give and take comes as second nature to you as a rule, this is not necessarily the way things are under present planetary influences. Patience is really necessary today.

11 SUNDAY *Moon Age Day 11   Moon Sign Sagittarius*

Holidays or trips of almost any sort are well accented now. Movement that is necessary for business purposes should also be quite useful and enjoyable. What won't be so good is finding yourself tied to the same spot as a result of having to do things simply because others tell you that you must.

12 MONDAY *Moon Age Day 12   Moon Sign Capricorn*

There are times today when it would definitely be a good thing to keep your own counsel. It isn't that you deliberately set out to interfere in a perceived situation, but more that what you say could be misconstrued. Taurus is quite capable of watching and listening without throwing any sort of spanner in the works.

13 TUESDAY *Moon Age Day 13   Moon Sign Capricorn*

The focus turns to leisure and pleasure and you clearly want to get as much fun from today as you can. This extends to others because it is now very important for you to lift one or two people out of the doldrums. Your social conscience is strong and you may be open to helping charitable causes at present.

14 WEDNESDAY *Moon Age Day 14   Moon Sign Aquarius*

Joint affairs of any sort are well highlighted for today. Such trends are especially useful in terms of business, but of course this might not be the case at all for you. You will want to spread your wings as much as possible during today and for the days to come, even if August is not holiday time for you.

15 THURSDAY   *Moon Age Day 15   Moon Sign Aquarius*

There is a strong emphasis now on broadening your horizons and on making sure you are in the right place at the right time to get ahead. Not everyone proves to be equally helpful today, but if you turn in the right direction, you can be sure of the sort of support you are looking for.

16 FRIDAY   *Moon Age Day 16   Moon Sign Aquarius*

Domestic responsibilities could so easily get in the way of things you would rather be doing. It pays dividends to think in advance and to make sure all those chores are out of the way so that you can concentrate on having fun. Compliments could be coming your way from unlikely directions.

17 SATURDAY   *Moon Age Day 17   Moon Sign Pisces*

Conversations of all kinds should be appealing today. When they are applied to your present business acumen, you should be able to get ahead in a very positive manner. There is quite a restless streak about you and there is no doubt that there are times you would rather be travelling than staying around to attend to responsibilities.

18 SUNDAY   *Moon Age Day 18   Moon Sign Pisces*

Your powers of attraction should be stronger than ever today. Compliments come from a host of different directions but nothing being said is likely to turn your steady Taurean head. Your intuition is strong, so you definitely know when someone is stringing you along, which could happen at this time.

19 MONDAY   *Moon Age Day 19   Moon Sign Aries*

There are many changes around just now and your greatest desire is to keep life on an even keel. Actually, it could be the case that you are trying too hard. Allow things to happen in their own good time. If you are constantly reacting, it is possible that you are not using either your intuition or your common sense enough.

20 TUESDAY
Moon Age Day 20   Moon Sign Aries

Keep on looking for those wide, open spaces. This is a holiday time generally, but turns out to be an especially good time for you to take a break. If you cannot get away from the rat race, at least leave some time free during the day. Even a walk in the park would be better than nothing.

21 WEDNESDAY
Moon Age Day 21   Moon Sign Aries

Your assertive nature now starts to show. This may come as a genuine surprise to some people and might be just what you need to wrong-foot the opposition. You won't take kindly to being told what to do, particularly in situations where you know you should be in the driving seat.

22 THURSDAY
Moon Age Day 22   Moon Sign Taurus

It's time to push ahead with your dreams and schemes because if you are going to make anything of them, this is the most likely period. Taurus is especially unsettled today, though not in a negative sense. All through the month, travel has been a distinct possibility and that eventuality is even more likely now.

23 FRIDAY
Moon Age Day 23   Moon Sign Taurus

This is a day during which you will find it possible to talk anyone into doing anything you wish. Your influence is extremely strong at this time and it isn't just because of the lunar high. You have been gradually increasing your persuasive ways to such an extent that you will have even most awkward people eating out of your hand.

24 SATURDAY
Moon Age Day 24   Moon Sign Gemini

An exchange of ideas and views could turn out to be very useful right now and there are plenty of people around who you could call on. In the end, probably the most unlikely person will be the one you choose, though you should definitely stay away from people who have difficulty in keeping their own secrets, let alone yours.

125

25 SUNDAY
Moon Age Day 25   Moon Sign Gemini

You have a bright, quick mind and remain determined to force situations to work out the way you would wish. Acting on impulse, something you rarely do, is a way to create a truly exciting Sunday. Personalities come into your life around this time and might bring new attitudes and modes of behaviour that you wish to adopt.

26 MONDAY
Moon Age Day 26   Moon Sign Cancer

Right now the key to success seems to lie with your career. You will need to deal with a few nagging details, even though these can be quite tedious at times, they could turn out to be significant. If you have a health concern try to avoid worrying too much about situations that may not be what they seem, but get expert advice.

27 TUESDAY
Moon Age Day 27   Moon Sign Cancer

This could be the high point of the month concerning travel and will see many Taureans packing their bags and jetting off somewhere or other. It doesn't really matter how near or far you go. The important thing is that you have worked hard of late and could do with a change of pace.

28 WEDNESDAY
Moon Age Day 28   Moon Sign Leo

A long-standing commitment could need urgent attention today. There is plenty on your agenda now, but if you spread your tasks a little, or even offload one or two of them on to willing volunteers, you will find the going easier. There are positive financial influences around that can be exploited.

29 THURSDAY
Moon Age Day 29   Moon Sign Leo

Press on with whatever activities you have planned and assume that things are going to work out the way you would wish. In the main, this is likely to be the case. This could be the best day of all for financial ventures and is also a notable period in terms of your overall popularity.

30 FRIDAY   *Moon Age Day 0   Moon Sign Virgo*

Life could take on a rather so-so quality today, unless you put in that extra bit of effort that can make all the difference. Don't be willing to accept second best, either from yourself or others. The urge to see new places is still around you and you might decide to make use of today to travel to see them.

31 SATURDAY   *Moon Age Day 1   Moon Sign Virgo*

Your sense of adventure grows and grows. Since it is likely you are not at work today, do something really different and make sure you have allies who can make the whole situation that much more enjoyable. Your general level of confidence isn't as high as it might appear, but you won't give any indication of this to others.

September 2019

1 SUNDAY
Moon Age Day 2   Moon Sign Libra

The emphasis falls on personal and domestic concerns today. Although there is still plenty going on in the outside world, you are taking less notice of it. Perhaps you want to set matters straight with someone in the family, or it could simply be that you realise how comfortable you are with life at home. Enjoy this mood.

2 MONDAY
Moon Age Day 3   Moon Sign Libra

A number of different necessities keep you busy and on the move. Significant progress should be the result, which itself leads to feelings of great satisfaction later in the day. At least a few hours now should be spent relaxing, probably in the company of people you haven't seen as much of as you would wish.

3 TUESDAY
Moon Age Day 4   Moon Sign Scorpio

If you feel somewhat burdened by situations, try to recognise the fact that part of the problem is the lunar low. It isn't easy to see things as clearly as usual while the Moon is in your opposite zodiac sign and you definitely do need to stand back and take a breather. Simply find ways to relax.

4 WEDNESDAY
Moon Age Day 5   Moon Sign Scorpio

The pitfalls you see before you now look deeper and more complicated than usual, but this is brought about by a state of mind. Once again it is important to allow yourself a longer-term view because even by tomorrow many situations will look different. Keep faith with your own abilities and let time pass.

5 THURSDAY   *Moon Age Day 6   Moon Sign Scorpio*

There could be one or two mishaps today, but you take them in your stride. In the main life should now be going pretty much the way you wish. There are occasions when you may have to disappoint someone, probably because of a clash of loyalties. Diplomacy is your middle name right now so use it wisely.

6 FRIDAY   *Moon Age Day 7   Moon Sign Sagittarius*

This might turn out to be the sort of day on which some of your most cherished ideals are being contradicted and questioned. The secret is to smile sweetly, if only because other people do have a right to their point of view. There is no need to worry because the planets suggest that you will get your own way in the end.

7 SATURDAY   *Moon Age Day 8   Moon Sign Sagittarius*

Others should be only too willing to lend you a hand today if you give them the chance. Socially speaking you should be on good form, with friends positively crowding round to show you their affection. Don't be too quick to judge the motivations of people you don't know very well because your judgement could be wrong.

8 SUNDAY   *Moon Age Day 9   Moon Sign Capricorn*

You probably won't be quite so sure of yourself today as has been the case recently. What you will have instead, though, is a greater degree of support, especially from family members and possibly your partner. Some unexpected people could rally to your defence regarding social issues later in the day.

9 MONDAY   *Moon Age Day 10   Moon Sign Capricorn*

Romance is likely to play a significant role in events today. Give some extra attention to your personal life, and start by telling your partner how important they are to you. Be prepared to enjoy what should be an active and very enterprising Monday, but don't take your eye off the ball in terms of work.

10 TUESDAY
Moon Age Day 11   Moon Sign Aquarius

There are likely to be new people coming into your life now and the planetary indications suggest that some of these contacts could turn out to be valued and trusted friends in the longer-term. Taurus is also playing in the major league as far as romance is concerned at the moment.

11 WEDNESDAY
Moon Age Day 12   Moon Sign Aquarius

If it is better financial circumstances you have been looking for, then this could turn out to be very much your period. It's true that the stars don't favour any special good luck at the moment, but most Taureans realise that with hard work and application they make their own luck. How true this is for you right now.

12 THURSDAY
Moon Age Day 13   Moon Sign Aquarius

Energy and determination won't be in short supply when you need them the most. There are planetary aspects around now that show how much you have to offer to social groups and your family. Friends should prove to be especially helpful and might have some news that could brighten your day no end.

13 FRIDAY
Moon Age Day 14   Moon Sign Pisces

You have it within you to bring out the best in others today, which has to be a good thing for a host of reasons. Firstly, you bring joy into the lives of the people you interact with. Second, and on a more personal level, you may be able to gain by having those people on your side. It's no sin to feather your own nest occasionally.

14 SATURDAY
Moon Age Day 15   Moon Sign Pisces

The pace of life is neither too fast nor too slow, which is the way you love things to be. Everyday matters that are important to you seem to be dealt with quickly, but that's not the same as enjoying the pace of the ride. Maybe just a little more drive and enthusiasm would turn out to be useful.

15 SUNDAY
Moon Age Day 16   Moon Sign Aries

Your sense of adventure is now present in great measure and you won't take kindly to being held back. You may even be rather more competitive than usual and could find yourself involved in some sort of competition. Taureans who have been a little out sorts of late should be feeling better now.

16 MONDAY
Moon Age Day 17   Moon Sign Aries

You could so easily find yourself in a prominent position today, so you will need to keep your wits about you. Being in the limelight is a double-edged sword for Taurus – you often like it, but sometimes you hate it at the same time. Fortunately, you should not be feeling particularly shy at present.

17 TUESDAY
Moon Age Day 18   Moon Sign Aries

You should now be feeling buoyed up physically and ready to face whatever challenges come your way. Although some Taureans could have been lacking in stamina in recent days, this looks likely to now be reversed. Challenges are something you will relish and the busier you are, the better you are likely to feel.

18 WEDNESDAY
Moon Age Day 19   Moon Sign Taurus

If this doesn't turn out to be a Wednesday to remember, you are probably not trying as hard as you could. All in all, the lunar high offers a mixture of possibilities during its September visit. On a personal level you appear to be attracting a lot of attention, while practical matters are dealt with in a flash.

19 THURSDAY
Moon Age Day 20   Moon Sign Taurus

Pottering around in the house won't be at all what appeals to you the most right now because it's clear you need to be getting out and about. Anything cultural is likely to appeal to you and the physical needs of your Earth-sign body also have to be kept in mind at the moment, so a long walk might be in order.

20 FRIDAY
Moon Age Day 21   Moon Sign Gemini

The pace of everyday life becomes quite rapid now, so much so that you don't really have time to stop and take a breath. Be specific when in conversation with others because if there is something you want, you need to ask for it plainly. Most people will respect your present honesty and integrity.

21 SATURDAY
Moon Age Day 22   Moon Sign Gemini

Your mind is sharp and your sense of humour certainly intact. This gives you the ability to get ahead of the game and to show the world what you are made of. In part this weekend is comprised of positive social encounters, most of which are geared towards improving your personal situation.

22 SUNDAY
Moon Age Day 23   Moon Sign Gemini

This is a good period for broadening your mind and for coming to new and quite revolutionary conclusions, sometimes about yourself. Keep an open mind with regard to the activities of certain friends, but don't be badgered into actions that genuinely go against the grain as far as you are concerned.

23 MONDAY
Moon Age Day 24   Moon Sign Cancer

A matter about which you have strong personal feelings could lead to you being put on the spot today. Unfortunately, you can't hide in the shadows regarding an issue that's important to you, so don't be afraid to speak your mind, even if you know others won't agree with your point of view. If you explain yourself, all should be well.

24 TUESDAY
Moon Age Day 25   Moon Sign Cancer

You will probably have your work cut out today trying to show people how much you care about them. In the end you might simply have to tell them one last time and leave it at that, because you can't allow the insecurities of others to govern your life. Enjoy being busy right now and some good financial prospects.

25 WEDNESDAY   *Moon Age Day 26   Moon Sign Leo*

This looks like being a busy period in most senses, though you should remember that a little rest is important too. Be prepared to go that extra mile for the sake of friends, and also take any proffered opportunity to travel. Confrontation with colleagues is not to be recommended at present.

26 THURSDAY   *Moon Age Day 27   Moon Sign Leo*

Lady Luck lends you a hand and should enable you to handle cash well. It should not be difficult to look ahead as you are in a shrewd and speculative frame of mind. There should be plenty of compliments coming your way, although this could lead to some confusion in your mind regarding the way others think about you.

27 FRIDAY   *Moon Age Day 28   Moon Sign Virgo*

Lively discussions seem to be the order of the day as September grows old. Keep your comments on any situation brief but honest and you won't go far wrong. Feelings of excitement might be somewhat justified by the promise of even better times to come, so you can afford to be optimistic.

28 SATURDAY   *Moon Age Day 0   Moon Sign Virgo*

This is a time of steady but relentless building, both in a financial and a personal sense, which should leave you feeling satisfied and happy. Trends also indicate that you should try not to fuss about details and stick to what you know when it comes to public discussions.

29 SUNDAY   *Moon Age Day 1   Moon Sign Libra*

Relationships might be anything but fun and games at the start of today, though matters ought to improve as the hours pass. Your powers of communication are still good so you ought to be able to talk yourself out of any difficulty. Your confidence isn't all it might be, but you should overcome this through competent action.

30 MONDAY   *Moon Age Day 2   Moon Sign Libra*

It should be easy enough now to get your own way with others.
There are people around who can be awkward to deal with as a rule,
but this doesn't appear to be a problem for the moment. Try not to
worry about upcoming events or situations; your chart indicates that
they could turn out to your advantage.

♉ October 2019

1 TUESDAY
Moon Age Day 3   Moon Sign Scorpio

Be prepared to take a back seat for the next couple of days. It isn't that you should feel forced to remain quiet on issues that you feel strongly about, but there wouldn't be any harm at all in simply taking a short holiday from making decisions. Allow others to do some of the jobs you don't like the look of.

2 WEDNESDAY
Moon Age Day 4   Moon Sign Scorpio

Events move slowly today and you will just have to accept this. It isn't that the lunar low is likely to depress you or cause any undue problems, but rather that the pace of progress now slows down so much that you realise the best way to deal with circumstances is to wait a while.

3 THURSDAY
Moon Age Day 5   Moon Sign Sagittarius

A few of the opportunities you have been expecting for a while are now likely to start turning up. Routines become less important to you at this time so you should feel free to experiment with new things. Some choices that under normal circumstances you would usually steer clear of could work out well today.

4 FRIDAY
Moon Age Day 6   Moon Sign Sagittarius

Keep discussions with others away from everyday matters and allow your mind to wander into the realms of the possible. You don't always daydream quite as much as you should because your practicality gets in the way. Now you can both talk – and perhaps write – as a visionary.

5 SATURDAY
Moon Age Day 7   Moon Sign Capricorn

Personal relationships should be working extremely well for you and some Taureans should be finding themselves at the start of exciting new romances. Even ordinary friends may be particularly warm towards you right now and some surprises could come from the direction of a really close pal.

6 SUNDAY
Moon Age Day 8   Moon Sign Capricorn

Although it won't be possible to do absolutely everything you would wish today, you can still find many ways to please yourself. Most important of all, you need to find moments – or hours – to get away from the mundane in life and into some sort of excitement, no matter what that might mean to you.

7 MONDAY
Moon Age Day 9   Moon Sign Capricorn

The more adventure you can get into your life, the greater the rewards. Don't be afraid of getting away from it all and accept almost any offer of a trip that comes along this week. There are people around who you haven't seen for some time and now is as good a time as any to rekindle what was once a bright flame.

8 TUESDAY
Moon Age Day 10   Moon Sign Aquarius

You are most likely happily on the go for most of today, with travel once again positively highlighted and an ability to make gains in new places. Organising yourself might prove a little awkward, though mainly in a humorous way. There is a tendency to be just a little absent-minded under present trends.

9 WEDNESDAY
Moon Age Day 11   Moon Sign Aquarius

Your present urge for independence is strong. As a result you can be somewhat restless and possibly rather headstrong. This is fine as long as you are aware of the fact and control it. What you definitely don't want to do today is to fall out with people who could prove useful later.

10 THURSDAY *Moon Age Day 12 Moon Sign Pisces*

Family and domestic matters are now highlighted in your solar chart. Although this won't prevent you from mixing with the rest of the world, the greatest gains to be made right now are around house and home. You may be feeling the need to plan the forthcoming weekend down to every detail but will need to accept changes to your plans if necessary.

11 FRIDAY *Moon Age Day 13 Moon Sign Pisces*

Your thinking and the way you communicate are positive. In the main you show a very humorous face to the world at large and there are likely to be many laughs along the way. Taurus occasionally takes itself rather more seriously than it should, though this definitely isn't the case now.

12 SATURDAY *Moon Age Day 14 Moon Sign Pisces*

This is a day during which you should be certain to keep your eyes wide open. With everything to play for and plenty of enthusiasm when it counts the most, you could be facing one of the most potentially successful periods of the year. Be sure to tell people the way your mind is working and leave nothing to chance.

13 SUNDAY *Moon Age Day 15 Moon Sign Aries*

The domestic scene is a busy place, with people coming and going all the time. Socially speaking your life is a buzz of activity and there are moments during which you will want to slow matters down a little. Your ability to get your message across is still extremely good.

14 MONDAY *Moon Age Day 16 Moon Sign Aries*

You can now afford to relax a little and improve your home life while you are about it. Commitment to practical issues at work might have to wait because for today at least you simply are not in the mood. Don't worry though because trends are going to change in an instant tomorrow.

15 TUESDAY *Moon Age Day 17   Moon Sign Taurus*

Your high spirits return, as does your sense of humour. Everything is a laugh today and even situations you once found hard going are dealt with in a flash. Most of the people you meet seem to be naturally compromising in their attitudes but much of this has to do with the way you are feeling yourself.

16 WEDNESDAY *Moon Age Day 18   Moon Sign Taurus*

Along comes the time of the month during which you can afford to push your luck a little. The gains that can come along today could surpass your expectations and you certainly do need to make quick decisions if you want to make the very best of life. Confidence is written all the way through you today.

17 THURSDAY *Moon Age Day 19   Moon Sign Taurus*

The brakes are still off, bringing a very positive and influential sort of Thursday. Although you are still motivated towards material success you should also find enough time to simply have fun. The bearing your attitude has on family members and particularly your partner is marked.

18 FRIDAY *Moon Age Day 20   Moon Sign Gemini*

This is a time during which love life and relationships should be putting a very definite smile on your face. If you don't have the time to do everything you wish in a practical sense, be willing to leave some of it for another day. Most of the people you meet today prove to be very reasonable.

19 SATURDAY *Moon Age Day 21   Moon Sign Gemini*

You are at your very best now in small gatherings, and especially so when mixing with people you already know. The slightly shyer quality of Taurus is on display and you also demonstrate a reserve that casual acquaintances might not understand. Nevertheless, in a professional sense, you still display confidence.

20 SUNDAY · *Moon Age Day 22 · Moon Sign Cancer*

Don't believe everything you hear today because trends suggest that there could be some confidence tricksters around. Be wary of anyone who is extremely charming and keep your guard up. Trends also indicate a slight tendency towards mysterious little illnesses today, although these look likely to be cleared up quickly.

21 MONDAY · *Moon Age Day 23 · Moon Sign Cancer*

Today could be a mixed bag, but is still likely to favour you in a general sense. If there are any frustrations, these are likely to come about as a result of the attitude of colleagues, some of whom are ploughing a very different furrow to your own. Keep abreast of things that are happening in your immediate locality.

22 TUESDAY · *Moon Age Day 24 · Moon Sign Leo*

Work and practical affairs keep you generally busy today and offer you the comfort of knowing that life is running in a smooth and steady way. There probably won't be too much in the way of excitement, though you aren't likely to be fazed by that at the moment.

23 WEDNESDAY · *Moon Age Day 25 · Moon Sign Leo*

Good times in relationships mark this period out as feeling safe, warm and generally comfortable. Although you can't count on the support of everyone you know, in the main the people you rely on the most come up trumps on your behalf. Concentrate on issues that can make you better off financially.

24 THURSDAY · *Moon Age Day 26 · Moon Sign Virgo*

You could discover that in financial matters you have to take a very patient point of view, which could make it difficult to be immediate in your approach. This can lead to some inner conflict because you really do want to get ahead today. Your creative potential remains essentially high, with some wonderful ideas coming along.

25 FRIDAY
Moon Age Day 27   Moon Sign Virgo

Although you could be feeling quite assertive today, you will still need to watch your step in some ways. Not everyone is working towards your ultimate good, no matter what they may say to the contrary. Problems are not likely to arise with relatives or friends, though colleagues could be more of a problem.

26 SATURDAY
Moon Age Day 28   Moon Sign Libra

Look out for problems regarding money. You need to be very careful what you spend today, and the things you spend it on. All in all, it might be best not to extend yourself financially at this point in time, but instead prefer to save and look ahead. However, trends indicate that you won't be too conservative in other ways.

27 SUNDAY
Moon Age Day 0   Moon Sign Libra

Getting out and about, away from routines, does wonders for your attitude at present. Outdoor pursuits would suit you fine, and you won't worry too much about what the weather decides to do. If circumstances keep you rooted to the spot, you will need to turn up the level of your imagination instead.

28 MONDAY
Moon Age Day 1   Moon Sign Scorpio

The lunar low indicates a period during which you might normally decide to take a rest, but there are astrological trends around now that make this less than likely. Don't try to start too many new ventures at this time and keep your efforts to a minimum when it comes to moving money from one place to another.

29 TUESDAY
Moon Age Day 2   Moon Sign Scorpio

Opportunities for material progress are going to be lacking today so you might as well decide to enjoy yourself in a social sense instead. You will want to focus most of your efforts on your partner, family members or really good friends. The world outside your own door probably doesn't hold that much fascination for you now.

30 WEDNESDAY   *Moon Age Day 3   Moon Sign Sagittarius*

Today should be reasonably fulfilling at work, though better still in terms of your social and personal life. Romantic opportunities may rear their heads on a number of occasions, particularly so if you look out for them. This might be a good time to buy someone a bunch of flowers or some other small gift.

31 THURSDAY   *Moon Age Day 4   Moon Sign Sagittarius*

The emphasis now is mainly on life's material pleasures and the sort of luxuries you have denied yourself recently. Be willing to allow yourself some pampering and don't be too quick to get things done. Whilst you are wallowing in the lap of luxury, your mind is working ten to the dozen.

November 2019

1 FRIDAY
☿ *Moon Age Day 5   Moon Sign Sagittarius*

Pressing emotional issues can be dealt with quite easily, even though you might get them out of all proportion at first. You are in sight of a potentially famous victory somewhere in your life and need only to keep going in the same direction you are following now. Friends should prove to be very supportive.

2 SATURDAY
☿ *Moon Age Day 6   Moon Sign Capricorn*

Your professional ambition is now much increased, leading you to thinking about work, even if you are not actually there today. A little confusion in the family is liable to lead to some very funny situations on a day during which your general sense of humour is already going off the scale.

3 SUNDAY
☿ *Moon Age Day 7   Moon Sign Capricorn*

Opt for a day of light relief if possible. You are in a state of mind that makes it impossible for you to take yourself or anyone else very seriously. There may be gains coming as a result of things you did in the past, which might cause you to look back and adopt a previous strategy again.

4 MONDAY
☿ *Moon Age Day 8   Moon Sign Aquarius*

Prepare for a useful period during which just about anyone you meet wants to offer the sort of help and support that is really what you need. Don't let your recent desire to do everything yourself get in the way of accepting a little assistance. If you do, there's a good chance you will upset someone who is important to you.

5 TUESDAY   ☿   *Moon Age Day 9   Moon Sign Aquarius*

Getting to grips with facts and figures might not be very inviting today but it could be necessary all the same. There are jobs to do that you really don't want to tackle, but in the end you will do them with good grace, probably early in the day in order to get them out of the way so that you can have fun.

6 WEDNESDAY   ☿   *Moon Age Day 10   Moon Sign Pisces*

Clear communication will be necessary if you want to enjoy a successful life at present. Make sure others know perfectly well what you are saying, and why. On another front, you might notice that there are many personal compliments coming your way, perhaps from interesting directions.

7 THURSDAY   ☿   *Moon Age Day 11   Moon Sign Pisces*

You can probably look forward to a little ego boost in social encounters because more compliments are likely to be coming your way. Under present circumstances this situation is hardly likely to turn your head but it is good to know that people notice you and want to be pleasant.

8 FRIDAY   ☿   *Moon Age Day 12   Moon Sign Pisces*

Throw negative thinking straight into a wastebasket and get on with living your life as positively as you can. Rules and regulations are almost certain to get on your nerves, even if you were originally responsible for instigating some of them yourself. It is really important that you find ways to enjoy this Friday.

9 SATURDAY   ☿   *Moon Age Day 13   Moon Sign Aries*

Compromises don't come easy to you now and you may have to try that little bit harder to deal with behaviour and attitudes you don't entirely understand. What you can be sure of today is that the future looks generally brighter and that you are now socialising more than of late.

10 SUNDAY ☿ *Moon Age Day 14   Moon Sign Aries*

A socially favourable day and one during which you can enhance your financial wherewithal simply by saying and doing the right things. Don't get stuck on specifics because it is the broad cross-section of life that matters at the moment. It might have occurred to you for the first time today that Christmas is coming!

11 MONDAY ☿ *Moon Age Day 15   Moon Sign Taurus*

There are few, if any, obstacles in your progress in life at the moment. The best of all worlds would find you responsive to change and anxious to follow situations through to their logical conclusions. If there are hurdles to overcome, now is the time to address them.

12 TUESDAY ☿ *Moon Age Day 16   Moon Sign Taurus*

Green lights are all around you and you are feeling positive and dynamic. Not everyone is in the same state of mind as you are, a fact that might mean leaving slower people to catch up later. Quick on the uptake and certainly anxious to make the most of romantic possibilities, the world is your oyster right now.

13 WEDNESDAY ☿ *Moon Age Day 17   Moon Sign Taurus*

Your own strengths and personal resources are now improving noticeably. There could be some benefactors about and even though these might not be the people you would expect, they are worth your attention. Bear in mind, that not everything that leads to a sense of personal success can be measured in financial terms.

14 THURSDAY ☿ *Moon Age Day 18   Moon Sign Gemini*

Work that requires careful thought or intelligence may now be highly rewarding, and communication is well highlighted in your solar chart. Both your mind and your heart can therefore be stimulated through new ideas and you are well able to offer good guidance to both associates and friends. Something you hear might confirm your suspicions regarding a colleague or acquaintance.

15 FRIDAY ☿ *Moon Age Day 19   Moon Sign Gemini*

Travel could be uppermost in your mind and if you are planning a long-term journey it might be sensible to speak to someone who knows the location well. Check and recheck all details before you embark. This is the best time of the week for conversation, even with people you have never met before.

16 SATURDAY ☿ *Moon Age Day 20   Moon Sign Cancer*

It is possible that you will find personal relationships to be quite demanding at present. Try to curb any tendency towards chemical dependency today, especially if you are a smoker or have been drinking rather too much of late. Taurus is sometimes given to excess, but it won't do you any good in the longer-term.

17 SUNDAY ☿ *Moon Age Day 21   Moon Sign Cancer*

Though certain invitations come your way this Sunday, there is something that makes you a less socially inclined animal for the moment. This doesn't mean you are avoiding other people but merely that at least part of your time is spent alone. Keep an open mind about some of your recently hatched schemes and ideas.

18 MONDAY ☿ *Moon Age Day 22   Moon Sign Leo*

Get routine jobs done as early in the day as you can, leaving you with more time later to have fun and to get on with the newest incentives that are coming into your life. Your confidence remains generally high so you should not hang back in any situation and you have it within you to really make much of this week go with a swing.

19 TUESDAY ☿ *Moon Age Day 23   Moon Sign Leo*

This is likely to be one of the best days of the month for being the centre of attention. This can be somewhat disconcerting for some Taureans, who can be shy on occasions. The attention that comes your way is definitely deserved so relax and enjoy the accolades.

20 WEDNESDAY ☿   *Moon Age Day 24*   *Moon Sign Leo*

Although you could register a slight lack of inspiration early in the day, it won't be long before you are feeling much more positive and really getting stuck into things. Avoid family disputes; in fact, it might be sensible to spend as much time as you can with people to whom you are not related at all.

21 THURSDAY   *Moon Age Day 25*   *Moon Sign Virgo*

Some helpful news is likely to be arriving very soon and you seem to be keeping in touch with as many people as possible right now. Your confidence remains high and there isn't much that is beyond your ability in a professional sense. For Taureans who are looking for a very romantic day, this one should not disappoint.

22 FRIDAY   *Moon Age Day 26*   *Moon Sign Virgo*

Don't listen to everything that is being said in your vicinity at present because a large percentage of it simply won't be correct. Misinformation can be the order of the day so it is very important that you continue to remind yourself that this is the case from time to time. Use your intuition when it comes to assessing newcomers into your life.

23 SATURDAY   *Moon Age Day 27*   *Moon Sign Libra*

Matters undertaken as part of a group give today an air of excitement and it is very easy for you to join in and have fun. Not everyone might appear to have your best interests at heart, but it is possible that in a few cases you are misinterpreting the situation. A better day for finances is possible with the chance of some unexpected gains.

24 SUNDAY   *Moon Age Day 28*   *Moon Sign Libra*

Although today should be generally settled, there could be some romantic tension about and this is something you would wish to avoid if at all possible. Give yourself time to relax, even though some practical matters might be pressing in on you. Above all, remember this is Sunday, which is supposed to be a day of rest.

25 MONDAY
Moon Age Day 29   Moon Sign Scorpio

A fairly sluggish day is on the cards and it might be difficult to get what you want from situations. To a great extent, you can blame the arrival of the lunar low. What won't help is to push on against all the odds. It would be far better to take a rest and come out fighting in a couple of days.

26 TUESDAY
Moon Age Day 0   Moon Sign Scorpio

This might be another day on which it will be impossible to get your own way in everything. Simply watch and wait, biding your time and laying down plans that you can action as soon as tomorrow. Your confidence might seem to be lacking at present but this is only a very temporary glitch.

27 WEDNESDAY
Moon Age Day 1   Moon Sign Sagittarius

Good fortune is highly likely to come from the direction of friendships today. You just can't get enough of your pals at the moment and will trust them implicitly. There are gains to be made as a result of efforts you made in the past and some interesting communications could be coming your way at any time now.

28 THURSDAY
Moon Age Day 2   Moon Sign Sagittarius

There are signs of new romantic developments on the way for at least some sons and daughters of Taurus. If you have been on the lookout for new love, this is a time when it could easily come along. Don't be too fixed in your attitude as far as work is concerned and be prepared to learn from those who are in the know.

29 FRIDAY
Moon Age Day 3   Moon Sign Capricorn

A selfish streak comes upon Taurus, which isn't at all typical of your zodiac sign. Try to keep it in check but at the same time realise that you can move forward as a result. In just about every sphere of your life the day is predominantly about balance and you need to be sure that yours is all it should be.

30 SATURDAY   *Moon Age Day 4   Moon Sign Capricorn*

A loved one or a family member requires fairly careful handling today, especially if they have recently had something of a rough ride. You will be in a good position to offer them a guiding hand. For your own part you are now definitely in the mood for fun and should know where to find it.

♉ ⑧
December
2019

1 SUNDAY
Moon Age Day 5   Moon Sign Aquarius

The most important thing today is keeping on top of organisational issues. While you should generally be feeling quite positive about life, you won't be very pleased with yourself if situations become confused or if you feel you are not living up to the expectations other have of you.

2 MONDAY
Moon Age Day 6   Moon Sign Aquarius

The spirit of teamwork is strong in you today and your ability to get on well with the world at large is more noticeable. Specific planetary trends show this to be a time during which Taurus becomes fascinated by the way things work. Some experimentation may be called for, if only to satisfy your curiosity.

3 TUESDAY
Moon Age Day 7   Moon Sign Aquarius

Any kind of teamwork remains rewarding and it looks as though you are becoming the life and soul of any party. Active and inspirational, you respond very well to changing circumstances and will now be more willing to actually bring a degree of uncertainty and even a little risk into your life.

4 WEDNESDAY
Moon Age Day 8   Moon Sign Pisces

Although friends could have a confused attitude towards specific situations, your own mind is crystal clear and you have little or no difficulty in organising yourself and others. The social whirl of Christmas might have started for you already, which would be no bad thing when you are feeling so positive.

5 THURSDAY   *Moon Age Day 9   Moon Sign Pisces*

Gathering together all the relevant information you need should be child's play now. You are particularly well organised at the moment, which is probably why others turn to you when they need sorting out. It might be necessary to fend off one or two social invitations, if only because you can't do everything.

6 FRIDAY   *Moon Age Day 10   Moon Sign Aries*

Certain sacrifices have to be made today if you want to get the very best out of any relationship. Although there are things you want to do, now may not be the right time to address them. You are spreading yourself quite thinly already and could probably do with offloading unnecessary tasks or information.

7 SATURDAY   *Moon Age Day 11   Moon Sign Aries*

What a good time this would be for having a chat with your partner, particularly on a deep and personal level. Present planetary trends favour a very sensitive and caring attitude on your part. An issue from the past could help you to solve a slight difficulty that exists at present.

8 SUNDAY   *Moon Age Day 12   Moon Sign Aries*

There are great rewards to be had from even the most mundane events now, though you will have to look at matters carefully and use a good deal of intuition to get the best from any situation. It might just be that you feel you cannot break through the carefully created shell of a colleague or friend.

9 MONDAY   *Moon Age Day 13   Moon Sign Taurus*

As the month advances, so you begin to realise with startling clarity that Christmas will soon be here. That won't be any problem today or tomorrow because you have more than enough energy to organise things. The lunar high makes you feel very positive about most situations now.

10 TUESDAY   *Moon Age Day 14   Moon Sign Taurus*

This is a high point in the month during which you are turning your attention towards plans you have been wishing to put into action for some time. Your general level of energy is high and good luck attends many of your efforts. Act now for maximum benefit in the days and weeks to come.

11 WEDNESDAY   *Moon Age Day 15   Moon Sign Gemini*

Although you might feel that your influence over everyday matters is rather limited, you would probably be wrong. Be willing to take a few chances and to push the bounds of credibility when it comes to your own ideas. Romance looms large in your thinking and compliments are not hard to come by.

12 THURSDAY   *Moon Age Day 16   Moon Sign Gemini*

In a social sense you should find yourself to be on the up. There are gains to be made from simply being in the right place at the right time and your instincts are well tuned at the moment. Friends should be extra supportive and you can also expect financial matters to take a turn for the better sometime around now.

13 FRIDAY   *Moon Age Day 17   Moon Sign Cancer*

You now excel as a social being and benefit from all kinds of activities that involve others. This is slightly different from the way Taurus sometimes is, so you may surprise yourself. You also have it within you to be lucky in love right now. A new relationship could be on the horizon for some.

14 SATURDAY   *Moon Age Day 18   Moon Sign Cancer*

You might have to sacrifice your own interests a little this Saturday in favour of thinking about the group. This may be family or it could be your friends but there is no doubt that you are very generous in your feelings and actions now. There are contrasts around you, not least of all in the way others behave.

15 SUNDAY   *Moon Age Day 19   Moon Sign Cancer*

You do well when you are in the limelight and when involved in any sort of group activity. It could be that Christmas has come early to Taurus, or merely that the present planetary happenings are encouraging you towards ever more social tendencies. These are good trends in which to feather your own nest professionally.

16 MONDAY   *Moon Age Day 20   Moon Sign Leo*

Avoid others getting hold of the wrong end of the stick by being willing to explain yourself early in the day. Clear communication is the key and can help you to avoid being disappointed by the outcome of any encounter. Business matters are now variable but in any case you might have other things on your mind.

17 TUESDAY   *Moon Age Day 21   Moon Sign Leo*

A great deal of what you do today could seem to be more trouble than it is worth. As a result you might decide that the time is right for a one-day holiday. That might be difficult because there are still things to be done before Christmas comes along. Don't worry – you will feel more like taking part tomorrow.

18 WEDNESDAY   *Moon Age Day 22   Moon Sign Virgo*

Differences of opinion are likely to crop up and there probably isn't very much you can do about the situation. Try to ignore people you don't like very much, rather than reacting adversely to them. Routines can be tedious right now and if this proves to be the case, find ways to sidestep them.

19 THURSDAY   *Moon Age Day 23   Moon Sign Virgo*

The time has come for a complete change of scenery and it is likely that the approaching holiday period will allow this. You may be tired of work, or at least certain aspects of it, and the upcoming break will give you an opportunity to think about things differently. Now is the time to get into festive mode.

20 FRIDAY
Moon Age Day 24   Moon Sign Libra

If you have expensive tastes you might get the opportunity to indulge them. Taurus is inclined to have a liking for the good life, as do all Earth signs, but you can also do without quite cheerfully if necessary. What seems to matter most right now is the affection coming at you from family members.

21 SATURDAY
Moon Age Day 25   Moon Sign Libra

You can't keep a good Bull down, and especially not right now. There are gains coming from very unlikely directions and before today is out the hint that things are looking up generally. You won't be at all shy when it comes to singing your own praises and will be generally popular with all sorts of people.

22 SUNDAY
Moon Age Day 26   Moon Sign Scorpio

Today brings the lunar low, but you don't have to allow that to prevent you from having fun. As long as you allow others to make the arrangements and the running, you can sit back and enjoy yourself immensely. However, you might not feel the need to move very far away from your own home.

23 MONDAY
Moon Age Day 27   Moon Sign Scorpio

You may feel slightly unlucky today, in which case it would be best not to chance your arm. Take the opportunity of this quieter time to relax a little. If you could find ways to cosset yourself, or maybe get the opportunity to sink into the lap of luxury, you will hardly notice the lunar low at all.

24 TUESDAY
Moon Age Day 28   Moon Sign Sagittarius

Christmas Eve arrangements might well be keeping you on the hop, but the sort of activities in which you are involved supply their own momentum. You won't believe everything you hear at present and will be determined to follow your own advice, especially in situations that involve finance.

25 WEDNESDAY *Moon Age Day 29 Moon Sign Sagittarius*

This Christmas Day should be a special one for you, mainly because of the many different opportunities it presents. It's true that some relationships could be slightly testing, though this is less likely if you keep the mood happy and light, especially around casual friends. If you get the chance to get out for a while today, take it.

26 THURSDAY *Moon Age Day 0 Moon Sign Capricorn*

Your social life and friendships seem to have all the support necessary now and you could be taking the opportunity to see people you don't get the chance to meet all that often. There are good trends around supporting the possibility of travel and you could easily get itchy feet if you spend too long in front of the television.

27 FRIDAY *Moon Age Day 1 Moon Sign Capricorn*

You are likely to be occupying a centre-stage position right now and would be willing to entertain others. This might not be what Taurus is about as a rule but you do have it within you now to be extremely showy. At heart, however, you are still as keen to look after your own life and circumstances as is always the case.

28 SATURDAY *Moon Age Day 2 Moon Sign Capricorn*

It is possible that you will be saying some things you don't really mean when involved in a romantic encounter. There could be a tendency for the Bull to be a little outspoken today, so try to avoid this if possible. Consideration is usually your forte but everyone has off days. Try to include someone who is lonely in your arrangements.

29 SUNDAY *Moon Age Day 3 Moon Sign Aquarius*

Financial opportunities are likely to work in your favour now and you will still be putting in plenty of effort. Whilst the rest of the world is going into New Year mode, you are still pitching away, as you will do until Tuesday. Don't be surprised if someone is setting you up as a sort of icon.

30 MONDAY
Moon Age Day 4   Moon Sign Aquarius

The second last day of the year marks a time during which getting your own way should be really easy. Lady Luck is with you, and might even lead you to think about the odd careful speculation. Routines won't interest you at all and you will be very pleased when the evening arrives and you can simply find bigger and better ways to enjoy yourself.

31 TUESDAY
Moon Age Day 5   Moon Sign Pisces

Make the most of the last day of the year. Get out and about as much as possible and certainly aim to have a really good time tonight. As for New Year resolutions, it might be best to leave those on the shelf for the moment. You will think more clearly about them once January actually arrives.

RISING SIGNS FOR TAURUS

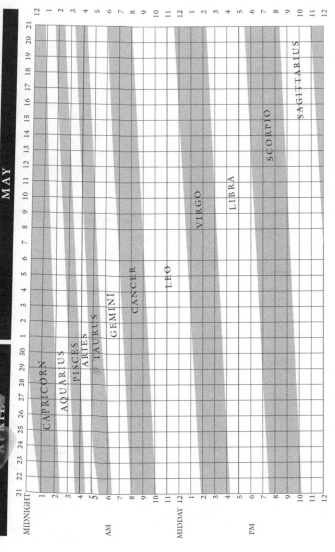

THE ZODIAC, PLANETS AND CORRESPONDENCES

The Earth revolves around the Sun once every calendar year, so when viewed from Earth the Sun appears in a different part of the sky as the year progresses. In astrology, these parts of the sky are divided into the signs of the zodiac and this means that the signs are organised in a circle. The circle begins with the sign of Aries and ends with Pisces.

Taking the zodiac sign as a starting point, astrologers then work with all the positions of planets, stars and many other factors to calculate horoscopes and birth charts and tell us what the stars have in store for us.

The table below shows the planets and Elements for each of the signs of the zodiac. Each sign belongs to one of the four Elements: Fire, Air, Earth or Water. Fire signs are creative and enthusiastic; Air signs are mentally active and thoughtful; Earth signs are constructive and practical; Water signs are emotional and have strong feelings.

It also shows the metals and gemstones associated with, or corresponding with, each sign. The correspondence is made when a metal or stone possesses properties that are held in common with a particular sign of the zodiac.

Finally, the table shows the opposite of each star sign – this is the opposite sign in the astrological circle.

Placed	Sign	Symbol	Element	Planet	Metal	Stone	Opposite
1	Aries	Ram	Fire	Mars	Iron	Bloodstone	Libra
2	Taurus	Bull	Earth	Venus	Copper	Sapphire	Scorpio
3	Gemini	Twins	Air	Mercury	Mercury	Tiger's Eye	Sagittarius
4	Cancer	Crab	Water	Moon	Silver	Pearl	Capricorn
5	Leo	Lion	Fire	Sun	Gold	Ruby	Aquarius
6	Virgo	Maiden	Earth	Mercury	Mercury	Sardonyx	Pisces
7	Libra	Scales	Air	Venus	Copper	Sapphire	Aries
8	Scorpio	Scorpion	Water	Pluto	Plutonium	Jasper	Taurus
9	Sagittarius	Archer	Fire	Jupiter	Tin	Topaz	Gemini
10	Capricorn	Goat	Earth	Saturn	Lead	Black Onyx	Cancer
11	Aquarius	Waterbearer	Air	Uranus	Uranium	Amethyst	Leo
12	Pisces	Fishes	Water	Neptune	Tin	Moonstone	Virgo